SHARING
GOD'S LOVE

SHARING GOD'S LOVE

by
Rosalind Rinker
and
Harry C. Griffith

ZONDERVAN
PUBLISHING HOUSE
OF THE ZONDERVAN CORPORATION | GRAND RAPIDS. MICHIGAN 49506

SHARING GOD'S LOVE
© 1976 by The Zondervan Corporation
Grand Rapids, Michigan

Fourth printing   March 1978
ISBN 0-310-32231-6

Printed in the United States of America

Contents

It is time we learned once again what it means to tell somebody else what Jesus Christ means to us as Lord and Savior in our lives. It is time for us to learn to expect that the Holy Spirit will teach us what to say when we don't know what to say so that we speak openly and boldly with great confidence about the glorious majesty of God, the great love of God revealed in Christ Jesus, and this holy fellowship brought about by the outpouring of the Holy Spirit.

— Bishop William H. Folwell
Diocese of Central Florida

Foreword

In recent years Christians have shown increased interest in evangelism and in their ability to witness to Jesus Christ. Still, there is a prevailing feeling that most people are not able to witness to God's love in a way that is natural to them. For that reason, the Task Group on Evangelism, composed of thirteen people, both lay and clergy, was formed by the Episcopal Diocese of Central Florida, and I was asked to join.

Members of the Task Group were people who had overcome their initial fear of witnessing but still weren't satisfied with "how to do it." Some had been through intensive training programs using various techniques for witnessing — from memorizing Bible verses to fit different situations to using printed material as a crutch to help them share Christ with others. Some had simply done the best they could without training, but with limited success.

Each person desired an effective, natural method for sharing God's love. Working toward that goal, we met together for four consecutive days. We began by being honest with one another and laying a foundation for loving one another. By the third day we were bringing personal requests into our prayer time, and a deep and lasting love given to us by God's Holy Spirit filled the room. It was beautiful.

The group questioned me extensively on the subject of witnessing and recorded it all on tape. Harry Griffith has a rare gift for organization, and soon sheets of newsprint and outlines papered our conference room. From these two sources, Harry put together this book. I edited it, but did not make many changes.

Preparing this book was a joyous new experience for me. It is not written in the first person as my other books have been. It is written in the "we" for several reasons. It is "we" because it represents the experiences of the thirteen others who worked with me, as well as my own. But it is also "we" because all of us are in the learning process: what applies in this book to the reader applies equally to those who wrote it. "We" are not trying to tell "you" what to do; we are sharing with you where we are and what we need to do to share the love of God more effectively in hopes that the principles involved will be useful to us all.

Special gratitude is expressed to the members of the Task Group for giving so much of themselves: Dick Bass, Dave Dillon, Bob Smith, Andrew Krumbhaar, Carole Ross, Fred and Rosa Barnes, Hap Merriman, Lorraine Renfroe, Frank Temple, George Keen, and Emily and Harry Griffith.

Wherever this book goes and whoever uses it, our prayers follow it that "silent believers" may become vocal witnesses in sharing the great love of God our Savior.

Rosalind Rinker

1 *Why Do It?*

1 *Why Do It?*

This book is written in the belief that all Christians want to share God's love with others. However, many things hamper us from witnessing.

1. We aren't confident that we know how to share God's love; thus, we feel inadequate or afraid.

2. We feel that it may be premature, or perhaps an invasion of privacy, to approach another person about Jesus Christ.

3. We don't know how to "break the ice" — that is, to turn from mundane subjects in a conversation to a meaningful discussion about the Lord.

4. We have vague subconscious fears about follow-up: "If I do help a person to discover Jesus Christ in his life, what do I do next?"

5. We think that to be an evangelist, one must have a driving, forceful personality.

6. We may believe that evangelism involves the ability to pull Bible verses out of a hat at the right moment — a verse or two for each of the multitudes of situations we might face. But how does one match the proper verse to the proper situation?

We could go on and on, because there are many reasons for

13

not sharing God's love with others. In fact, there is only one reason for doing it: *Jesus told us to do it!*

Our Lord did not tell us how to share God's love in every situation we might face, but it is clear from reading the Gospels that He did expect His people to go forth and proclaim the Good News of God's salvation in whatever circumstance He would prepare for them. Equally important (and this is one reason why He promised the gift of the Holy Spirit), our Lord has encouraged His people to share His love in ways that are natural to them.

That is one purpose of this book: to help people see how they may share God's love in ways natural to them.

The second purpose of the book is to show that basically there are only seven types of people with whom we need to learn to talk about Jesus Christ. We will come into contact with countless people in our lifetime, and, to a degree, every person in this world is as different from every other person as his fingerprints. But if we can learn some of the principles that apply to these seven categories of persons, we will be able to share God's love more effectively with the hundreds of people we meet.

A few matters should be understood at the outset, however. First, we need to understand what our responsibility is and what God's responsibility is in the ministry of evangelism, because it is a shared ministry. We can be most thankful that we don't have to do it "on our own."

1. *It is our responsibility to believe that in Jesus Christ we have the Answer all men should seek* — even though they may appear to prefer an entirely opposite one. If we do *not* feel that we have the Answer (in our relationship with Christ), then we need to engage in prayerful self-examination, and discover what is lacking in our relationship with Him. We cannot proclaim what we do not have; we cannot bear witness to what we ourselves do not believe.

2. *It is God's responsibility to prepare the hearts of those with whom we would share Jesus Christ.* If we do what is expected of us and the

14

person with whom we talk does not respond in a positive way, that is God's problem, not ours. It is God's problem because the timetable is God's, not ours. He may only want us to "sow seeds" within the person — seeds that He will later use as part of the total process of preparing that person to receive Jesus Christ as Lord and Savior. It may take the loving concern of 20 Christians to reach an individual, and we may be number 13 on the list! On the other hand, if someone does respond positively to our presentation of Christ, we need to remember that it is because God has prepared his heart, not because we have cleverly notched another soul on our spiritual belt.

3. *It is our responsibility to take the risk, to be vulnerable, to be willing to fail in trying to share God's love.* We may be ridiculed or even rejected for our faith in Christ. We are not guaranteed immunity from that. In fact, we are promised quite the opposite! Jesus said, "If any man would come after me, let him . . . take up his cross daily and follow me." Our availability and obedience to God's will is our "cross." It is not an option.

4. *It is God's responsibility to redeem our honest mistakes.* He asks not for our ability, but for our availability, and He uses our willingness to proclaim Christ, no matter how inadequate or imperfect that proclamation may seem to us. Moreover, God, in His power, can transform even our failures at sharing His love into instruments of victory. Just as God's timetable is not ours, neither are His ways ours. He uses us, however, because we are all He has chosen to use.

5. *It is our responsibility to prepare to share God's love with the seven types of people we will meet.* Jesus said that the Holy Spirit would guide us in what to say as we proclaim Him, but that does not mean we simply open our mouths and God speaks (although that does happen sometimes!). Christian evangelism is a cooperative venture; God certainly does His share, but He rightfully expects us to do ours.

6. *It is God's responsibility to lead the person to Jesus.* Although we may be the instrument through which the person wants to accept Jesus as Lord and Savior, God has prepared his heart

and He will — by His Holy Spirit — bring about that accept-ance of Christ on the part of the individual.

7. *Finally, it is our responsibility to be guided by the Holy Spirit as we share God's love with others.* We should not program ourselves to say and do certain things in certain situations. Rather, we should continually seek God's guidance about what to say and when to say it. Let's forget techniques and arguments — that's not God's way. If we are truly willing to share Christ with others and have prepared ourselves to do so, then God will guide us, gently but clearly, in what to do, how to do it, and when to do it. If, however, we begin to feel the urge to ram our message down someone's throat, we can be sure it is not God who is guiding us, but Satan who is trying to interfere and make our work ineffective.

It would seem, then, that God has only three responsibilities, while we have four; yet consider the weight of responsibility He carries compared to what we shoulder. God (1) prepares the hearts of those with whom we would talk, (2) redeems our mistakes, and (3) leads those persons to accept Christ. We only have to (1) believe that Jesus is the Answer, (2) be willing to say so, (3) do some preparation in how to say so, and (4) be guided by the Holy Spirit in doing so. As always, God makes our burdens relatively light.

The second matter we need to understand is what we mean when we say we should share God's love in ways that are natural to us. What do we mean by "natural"?

For one thing, we mean relax! There is no single right way to proclaim Jesus Christ to another; there are no set steps to be taken in perfect sequence, no "right set" of Scripture verses that must be used at the proper time. The more we become con-cerned about technique, the less we will be free to share God's love.

There are only three things that a Christian needs to know how to do in a way that is natural to him: (1) how to show someone that God loves him; (2) how to tell a person who Jesus Christ is and why that person should believe in Him; and (3)

16

how to show that person that his life can be changed by believing in Jesus Christ. God asks us to do this in the most effective way that accords with our personality, our capabilities, our situations, and our knowledge of our faith at any given point in time; and that is what is meant by "natural."

Certainly there are relatively few of those many people we meet with whom we will be able to accomplish items 2 and 3 above in any depth. But there are multitudes of ways in which we can share God's love and witness to our personal relationship with the Lord Jesus Christ. However, if this is not done in a natural way, we will simply be projecting a contrived image of Christ, and that won't help anyone.

In any discussion we may have with a person who is not a committed Christian, we have not witnessed until we have consciously found a way to mention Jesus Christ in a manner meaningful to that person. Here, of course, we are talking about those contacts resulting in some reasonable degree of discussion; we do not go so far as to say that we should hold up the line at a ticket counter to talk with the cashier about Christ simply because she is someone with whom we have come into momentary contact. However, if we look for them, most of us will have numerous opportunities each day to share Christ in a significant way.

A Christian should regard even an idle conversation as a possibility for presenting the name of Jesus Christ. Often people make statements in our presence that deny Christ, such as, "All we need to do to correct the terrible situation in our country is to get back to sound morals and ethics." If we allow such a statement to pass without bringing the name of Christ into it, we have missed an opportunity God has made available to us.

Rosalind told us that she has made this covenant with God: Whenever she is alone with another person, she will try to bring Jesus Christ into the conversation in a relevant way. Sometimes she may only have the opportunity to say, "God loves you." Yet this is what it is all about, and it certainly is a meaningful message to give someone who needs to know that God does love him. Further, as we will see in subsequent chapters, there are simple, wordless motions, reactions, and attitudes the Christian can use to show a person that God loves him.

We are not being led, through this book, to become "street corner evangelists"; we are not being asked to knock on doors or buttonhole people, but to develop a life style — an openness, an attitude, a willingness — of sharing God's love with those persons with whom we come into contact.

Leading a person to a commitment to Jesus Christ is but a first step in that individual's Christian life. He then needs to be brought into a warm and loving fellowship of Christians where he may be nurtured in the faith and given an opportunity to serve God. Therefore, the natural person for us to be telling about God's love is the one who might be led into that Christian fellowship of which we are already a part. It would behoove us, then, to know something about the manner in which our church expresses, through worship and teaching, the facts of God's love we are called upon to share. However, it is Jesus to whom we are pointing the individual, not the church!

Finally, none of the training in this book will be of any value unless it is put into practice. As we learn, through studying this book and through any practical training we may do in connection with it, it is essential that we immediately begin to share God's love with others as such opportunities are provided. Then as we progress, we will not be talking theory, but fact. All of us know, through personal experience, the practicalities and problems of the study we are pursuing. The one who is unwilling to put the principles of this book into practice as soon as possible after he discovers them would do better to close this book now and put it aside. However, those who are willing to accept the opportunities God gives are on the verge of a life-changing experience as they come to know more and more about how to share God's love in a sick and weary world.

Before we go further, then, let us resolve to be willing to share God's love and commit ourselves to upholding our end of this shared ministry. Let us also commit ourselves to letting people know that God loves them by trying to bring Jesus Christ into our conversations in a meaningful way, or, failing that, to be willing to express to others the fact of God's love in attitudes, actions, and words. Finally, let us be willing, in ways that are natural to us, to tell others who Jesus Christ is, why they should believe in Him, and how their lives can be changed by believing in Him. These are the things we should have in mind as we come into contact with the "seven people."

Study Assignment

Write, in your own words, what you believe you are called to do as an evangelist.

2 *The Seven People*

2 *The Seven People*

Each of us will come into contact with countless people during our lifetime. If we try to think in terms of evangelizing every one of them, we are faced with an overwhelming task and can easily reject it outright. But if we realize that there are only seven types of people with whom we will be called upon to share God's love, and that we are given adequate instruction in how to share Christ with those seven types, it looks like an easier job.

And who are these people? Briefly, here are the seven categories of persons with whom we could be expected to share God's love.

1. *The person who "invites an invitation."* This is the person who comes to us and says, "I want to accept Jesus Christ as my Lord and Savior." We probably won't meet many people like this, but if we are open in our Christian walk and show forth Christ in our own lives, we will encounter a few of them. Something may have happened in their lives through which Christ has become real and they want to know how to accept Him as Lord and Savior. Our role is to insure that this person understands the step he is taking and to lead him through it.

2. *The person who shows an interest in us, in our church, or in Christ.*

This individual is not necessarily ready to accept Jesus Christ, but he is interested. He is interested in us and in what is "different" in our Christian lives, or he is interested in our church and what it would mean to become a member of it. As with Person No. 1, he may be attracted directly to Jesus Christ and want to know more about Him. Again, we want to be sure the person gets the information he desires, and, if appropriate, we would like to lead him into a commitment of his life to Jesus Christ.

3. *The uninterested friend or relative.* Many feel this is the most difficult person to whom to show the love of God. Some have said, "Don't even try to show this person Christ; get someone else to do it." There are, however, ways in which we, as Christians, have an obligation to share God's love with our uninterested friend or relative. When we say "uninterested," we mean that the friend or relative shows no interest in Jesus Christ, in our church, or in our relationship with Christ. As we shall see when we study Person No. 3 in depth later, there may be special reasons for his lack of interest, and we must deal with those factors if we are to help him.

4. *The uninterested neighbor.* Because this individual is not necessarily a friend, we place him in this category instead of into the category of Person No. 3. The uninterested neighbor knows how we live; he can hear the members of our family quarreling with one another from time to time, or knows what other bad habits we have. There are special problems in dealing with him, as well as special opportunities to reach him.

5. *The person with whom we come into contact.* This is not the girl at the ticket counter with whom we have no reasonable opportunity for discussion. Rather, it is the individual with whom we come into contact for some period of time. He may be someone with whom we work (although we have not become friends) or the service station attendant whom we see two or three times a week. That is, he may be someone with whom we come into contact on a regular basis. On the other hand, he may be a person we sit beside on a lengthy trip. He may have some data

about us because of previous contacts or his data may be gained from our opening conversation with him as we share a tiny segment of our lives together.

6. *The person who opposes what we believe about Christ.* This individual is not uninterested. He is interested, but in a negative way. He may truly resent what we stand for as a Christian. On the surface, he may seem to be the most difficult person with whom we would come into contact. In reality, however, he is probably much closer to Christ than the apathetic person in categories 3, 4, and 7 (and perhaps 5). This individual has needs, and any contact is certainly an opportunity to move him toward Christ.

7. *The nominal Christian.* Most people would agree that this individual, along with Person No. 3, is in the "extremely difficult" category. If asked in a survey what his religious affiliation is, he calls himself a Christian, although he has no personal relationship with Jesus Christ. We must be careful, however, about assuming that other people are only nominal Christians. Many people fall into varying degrees of this category, and our purpose here is not to argue who is and who is not a "nominal Christian." Our purpose is to learn how to share God's love.

In addition to the seven people, there are three special categories of people that deserve some individual consideration: (1) a husband or wife who either is not a Christian or is only a nominal one, (2) our children while they are still a part of the family unit, and (3) the person who has an obvious need (physical, mental, etc.), regardless of which of the seven categories he might fit.

Many of the principles that apply to one person will also apply to several others. Therefore, we cannot study any one of the seven people in isolation from the others. Accordingly, we should develop not only an understanding concerning each principle that applies to one or more people with whom we will have an opportunity to share God's love, but also a knowledge of those special opportunities, problems, and other factors that

25

apply to each of the seven people. In so doing, we are "doubly trained" to handle any situation we may face. Further, we can always fall back on the fact that any circumstance we do face is one which God has either created or has allowed to happen. He will give us courage and guidance if we have prepared ourselves and are open to the leading of His Holy Spirit.

Now, having been introduced to the seven persons, let us try to understand them more fully.

Study Assignment

Do one of the following exercises:

1. List one or more persons (by name, if possible) who, for you, fall into each of the seven categories.

2. Prayerfully make a list of people whom God has shown you are persons with whom you should share His love. Next to each name, note which of the seven categories is appropriate.

Person No. 1

3   *One Who "Invites an Invitation"*

Person No. 1

3 *One Who "Invites an Invitation"*

As we have already mentioned, Person No. 1 is the individual who is ready to accept Christ as his Lord and Savior. He has discovered Christ through reading a book, through the changed life of a friend or loved one, or during worship services on Sunday morning. He simply wants to know what he needs to do to become a Christian. We want to be sure he knows what he is doing in taking this step, and we want to help him take it.

How do we deal with the person who is ready to commit his life to the Lord when he comes to us and says, "I want to take this step"? It will be an uncommon occurrence, but it will happen; and there are many who believe it will be happening more frequently in the days ahead. We will have those opportunities, particularly if we are open to them.

In a real sense, Person No. 1 is the easiest person with whom we will have an opportunity to share God's love. He is ready. He has already accepted Christ in his heart, and we simply need to be the instrument through whom God "seals the promise." However, we are going to spend more time discussing Person No. 1 than any other individual in our study because there are basic principles which apply to our talking with him that are common to each of the other six persons. We will deal with those principles now so we may have them in mind as we consider the other people with whom we will come into contact.

With Person No. 1, as with anyone else, we need to find out "where he is" and if he truly knows what he is doing in offering his life to the Lord. We should take the time to cover several critical points with him rather than being overly eager to "bring him into the fold." We do not want to quench the Spirit by belaboring points or dragging out theology when the person is ready to make a simple commitment of faith. However, we want it to be clear to him that he is committing his life to Jesus Christ as Lord and Savior and not simply reacting to some religious experience which may not even be Christian in nature. The individual needs to know who Christ is and what He did for us.

The first step in the process involves a willingness and an ability to listen. Listening may well be the most neglected aspect of the evangelical ministry. We have something to say in sharing Jesus Christ with others, but that carries with it an obligation to do a great deal of listening. Otherwise, we end up answering questions that have never been asked and professing beliefs that the individual is either unable or unwilling to comprehend. We would do well to remember that God, in His wisdom, gave us two ears and one mouth.

There are two aspects of listening we should consider. The first is simply giving the other person an opportunity to say what Jesus Christ means to him and why he wants to commit his life to Christ. That is what we would call simply "hearing the person out." Sometimes, however, the person needs to be stimulated to reveal his inner feelings about a matter so personal as his desire to give Jesus priority in his life. Then, if "simple listening" does not produce evidence that the individual knows what step he is taking, we should apply the principle of gentle probing and questioning so he has an opportunity to develop his own thoughts.

If the person comes to us, knowing we are Christians, and says he wants to commit his life and asks how to do it, we want to be sure he knows to Whom he wants to commit his life. Therefore, we would ask a question such as, "What do you know (or believe) about Jesus Christ?" Or if he comes to us with a desire to give his life to God and then says, "How does Christ fit into all of this?" we can turn the question back to him by saying, "What does Jesus Christ mean to you?" By this gentle probing, we learn exactly where the individual is in his understanding of Jesus Christ.

There are no principles in this book more important than those with which we have just dealt. We shall come back to them continually as we study the other six people and as we look at how particular conversations can develop in talking with others about Christ. Therefore, we cannot emphasize too strongly the need to give the other person an opportunity to develop and express his thoughts, questions, doubts, prejudices, opinions, and other areas of concern so we can know, to the extent it is knowable, exactly where he is before we seek to enlighten him.

As we talk with Person No. 1, we may find either that he (1) does not know who Jesus Christ is and why he should believe in Him, or (2) he has not seen how his life can and will be affected by believing in Jesus Christ. The first possibility can happen because he has had an experience with God without being able to see the essentiality of Jesus Christ within that experience. The second can occur as a result of something that has been purely an emotional experience from which the individual sees no implications for change in life style. That is why it is extremely important to clarify these issues for the individual while supporting his enthusiasm for the step he wants to take.

Much wasted time and just plain "bad witnessing" goes on as a result of our readiness to give pat answers to questions not being asked. So, we must take the time to listen, gently probe, and turn questions back to the individual. We should give him the opportunity to fully express where he is before we begin showing him how to get where he wants to be.

This is probably a good time to consider how to deal with

enthusiasm. We should do all we can to avoid dampening the enthusiasm of the individual who has come into an experience with God. Virginia Lively, an evangelist in her own right, tells the story of her husband's first visit to a farm when he was a boy. After being out in the barnyard for a short time, he came running into the kitchen with something behind his back and said to his aunt, "Guess what? I was just out there where all those chickens are and heard one of them making a lot of noise as it got up from the hay. And guess what I found where that chicken had been?" He beamed as he brought his "prize" from behind his back. "Oh," she said, "it's only an egg."

Imagine how the boy's enthusiasm was dampened by that reaction! How many times have we done a similar disservice to the individual who has had a genuine experience with God and has come to share it with us in that bright, shining spirit of the first glimmer of God's love?

We should realize the need to support the new Christian in his enthusiasm while helping him to get it into perspective. But *only* if he knows we share with him a profound gratitude to God for the dramatic revelation he has experienced can we help the individual put that experience into proper alignment in an effective manner.

To recap, then — we want to share with enthusiasm the experience of God the individual has had. In doing so, however, we want to lead him into a fuller understanding of it. Therefore, we may need to develop with him who Jesus Christ is, why he should believe in Him, and how his life can and will be changed by believing in Christ. Each is an important topic and will be dealt with separately in the following chapters.

Study Assignment

Write out what you did at some time in the past when a Person No. 1 came to you. (Or if that never happened, write out what you would have done.) Now, note what you would do differently, having read chapter 3.

Person No. 1

4 *The Testimony*

4 *The Testimony*

We have noted that it is our obligation as Christians to be able to tell a person who Jesus Christ is, what He did, and why we should believe in Him. We also have an obligation to be able to tell a person how his life can and will be changed, and the best way of doing that is to be able to share the ways in which our lives have been changed and are being changed daily as a result of our relationship with Christ. For the purposes of this book, we will use the term *witness* in reference to telling another who Christ is (Acts 1:8) and the term *testimony* to connote the means by which we tell another about Jesus Christ in our own lives. The latter is the subject of this chapter.

In talking with Person No. 1, it is quite possible that he will have so complete an understanding of who Christ is and how Christ can change his life that it is not necessary to give him either a witness or a testimony. However, for the reasons previously stated, we should be prepared to do so. Further, we should have both our witness and our testimony ready, as appropriate, in talking with each of the six people who follow.

What, exactly, is a *testimony?* Normally, a Christian's testimony involves telling another person what his life was like before he met Jesus Christ, how he came to know Jesus Christ in a personal way, and how his life has changed and is changing daily as a result of his relationship with Christ.

We all have (or should have) stories about what God has done in our lives. For example, we may have had a disagreement with a friend, resulting in a cooling of our relationship. Later there was a healing because God showed us how our differences could be resolved. When someone else has a similar problem, we then are able to share with him how God helped us in that situation.

The following sample testimonies, necessarily abbreviated in nature, may be helpful:

I am from a traditional, conservative background. I was baptized and confirmed in the Episcopal church, but spent my Sunday school days in a Baptist Sunday school, for it was closer than the Episcopal church. Somehow I had always believed that God had a plan for everyone's life, and I was pleased with the one He had worked out for me. Being a "religious" person by nature, I had always liked to go to church, pray, and read the Bible. After I was married, my deepest desire was that my husband would become an Episcopalian and love the church as much as I did.

When he was finally confirmed, he became not only an Episcopalian, but a Christian as well. This frightened and threatened me terribly, for I gradually began to realize that I was dangerously close to worshiping the church and not our Lord. I found that I had to set aside all my preconceived notions of what Christianity was and literally start all over. My prayer was: "Lord, I thought I knew You; I thought I understood what Christian love was, but I guess I don't, so please teach me." And He did!

First of all, He showed me that sin could include bitterness, resentment, and getting your feelings hurt over nothing. He showed me that I had never felt the burden of sin in my life and that I was a Pharisee.

As all of this was going on, I met an Episcopal priest's wife who asked me if I had ever made a personal commitment to Jesus Christ. My reply was, "I've tried." Then she asked me to give as much of myself as I could to as much of God as I understood. I made a tiny commitment that day, but six weeks later I asked God to take the rest. Just after that confession of faith, I made a confession of sin which really set me free and opened the door of faith.

In six months' time, my husband and I found ourselves in full-time

Christian work, which still amazes and astounds me.

I have found, and am finding daily, more and more freedom in the Lord. I still do lots of sinning, failing, and falling, but He is always there to pick me up. As I walk with Him, I find there is always more to know and love about our Lord Jesus.

*   *   *

It is difficult for me to remember when I did not know Jesus Christ; I feel I always have. I was brought up in a devout Presbyterian family where there was daily Bible reading and a close relationship to Jesus Christ and His church wherever we happened to be living. When I was ten years old, my parents took me to hear an evangelist speak at our church in Atlanta. I do not remember his message, but I do remember that there was an altar call, and I went forward and received Jesus as my Savior.

Fortunately, there was never a falling away from my faith in college years, and, in answer to my mother's prayers, I married a Christian. Through the ups and downs, the tragedies and joys of many years of marriage – plus bringing up two children – the Lord was always there when I needed Him. He was my Rock to lean on; and during those times when I felt He was all I had, His grace was always sufficient. We attended church regularly; I taught Sunday school for several years, and I read my Bible as my Christian duty. Nevertheless, I knew something was missing – I was not growing spiritually as I continued to strive on my own, never abandoning my own self-centeredness.

Then several years ago I discovered what was wrong in my Christian walk – the power of the Holy Spirit dwelling in me had never been released. So, at the end of a teaching mission I went forward again – this time to turn myself completely over to Jesus and to ask Him to fill me with His Holy Spirit. I gave Him all my life to do with as He pleased, and I asked Him to be my Lord as well as my Savior.

Then things began to change. The Bible came alive, my prayer life blossomed, and I was filled with great joy and love – which could come only from the Holy Spirit. I now knew Jesus in a different way. I could talk to Him and ask Him to take away all the emotions I could not handle – resentment, envy, jealousy, fear, and all the rest. I began to understand about forgiveness and how I needed to forgive others before I asked Jesus to forgive my sins. I began to see His healing all around me – the beautiful healing of families and all relationships, as well as the healing of illnesses of mind, body, and spirit. There was a lot of cleaning up that Jesus needed to do in me and that process is still continuing. But now I know real

37

freedom in the Lord Jesus, and a whole new dimension has opened up in knowing and experiencing God's love in Christ Jesus.

* * *

How great is God!
It was not until I consciously realized that I, a sinner, had personally put Jesus Christ on the cross that I began to experience the love and presence of God in my daily life. I have received much guidance and inspiration through the years since then, and He has changed my negative habits into positive ones. In the midst of many difficult circumstances and much personal sorrow, I have found the greatest thing that has happened to me is knowing the reality of the presence of our Lord Jesus Christ in the midst of all the happenings of life and knowing life eternal in the "now."
Thanks be to God!

Obviously, testimonies will vary just as people vary. However, there are some common threads of truth running through all of them. Often a crisis of some sort has caused a person to face up to his lack of a relationship with Christ, and that has either immediately or ultimately led to his decision to accept Christ. In some testimonies there is evidence of guilt which resulted in confession and forgiveness, but we should not assume that our testimony *has* to be one of the guilt-ridden sinner who has been saved. In fact, some people come to the Lord through the realization of His abundant love either over a period of time or in a particular crisis they have faced.

A testimony should reflect the ways in which our life style has changed through our relationship with Christ, but we must be careful not to come across in a self-righteous, look-how-great-I-am-now manner. Further, a complete testimony should show how God is changing us day by day. If that is not a natural part of our testimony, we need to examine what is wrong in our daily walk with the Lord that prevents our having a living testimony.

The only way to have a testimony is to prepare it and then use it. We should write our testimony on paper, using the guidelines given above. Then we should go over it (giving it verbally, as opposed to reading it from the sheet) with a Christian friend who is capable of critiquing it. Finally, we should pray for the opportunity to give our testimony so that it can become a real part of our life as a Christian.

Our testimony represents a major portion of the preparation we need for an encounter with anyone.

Study Assignment

1. Write out your testimony.

2. Present it aloud (don't read it) to a Christian friend and let him critique it for you. If you are studying this book as a group, divide into twos and each give your testimony.

3. Pray that God will lead you to someone who needs to hear your testimony.

Person No. 1

5 *The Witness*

Person No. 1

5 The Witness

Many Christians do not understand that they have an obligation to present Jesus Christ at the appropriate time to the person who has never met Him. Lay people tend to think that a presentation of Christ is too theological and that an "untrained layman" would make many mistakes in trying to do so. Clergy, on the other hand, quite properly feel it is lay people who should be able to lead other lay people into a relationship with Jesus Christ. They would argue the old adage, "Shepherds don't make sheep; sheep make sheep."

In the first chapter of this book, we dealt with the fact that God prepares the hearts of those with whom we share, redeems our mistakes, and leads those people to accept Christ. We don't have to be theologians. We simply have to be obedient. It does not mean standing on a street corner or hiring an evangelist to come into the church. It is simply sitting down and chatting, person to person, about what Jesus means to us. We don't preach; we just give the nonbeliever something to believe in about Jesus Christ. This chapter deals with our preparation to witness to who Jesus is, what He did, and why a person should believe in Him.

How can we explain to a non-Christian who Jesus Christ is? By presenting "the gospel according to us": what we understand about Jesus and why He came to live among us, die on a cross, and be raised from the dead. It should be based on what we know from our study of the Bible, as limited as that study may be at this particular time. It may include specific quotations from Scripture. It may be illustrated, and probably should be, by drawing on a blackboard or the back of an envelope so that the message has a lasting visual effect on the mind of the person to whom we present it. But, as we have mentioned numerous times, it should be a presentation that is natural to us.

As with the testimony, the witness will vary greatly from person to person. What is important to one person in the life, death, and resurrection of Christ is less important to another and vice versa. God will use the presentation that is meaningful to us to reach the person to whom we present it.

What is the importance of being able to quote Scripture when we are witnessing? Obviously, it is helpful to know appropriate passages of Scripture; however, it is not essential. In fact, sometimes a person can do too much "Scripture quoting" in his witness. We want the person with whom we share God's love to see that God is real to us in our lives. Too much "Scripture quoting" may seem like going to secondary sources to back up what we have to say. So, although it is good to be able to quote Scripture to emphasize points, we must be careful not to overdo it.

As is also true with the testimony, there are certain threads of truth that will run through almost every witness. For instance, we will probably want to show why it was necessary for God to manifest Himself in Jesus Christ in order to reach man; why it was necessary for Christ to die on a cross; why He was raised from the dead and lives forever (offering us eternal life with Him); and what specific benefits (or promises) we have received as a result.

To help us visualize our witness, here are several examples of witnesses presented by other people. We would caution against simply adopting one of the following as our own; rather, we should work out a witness that is natural to us. However, the examples should encourage us to see that it can be done, for these were prepared by lay people who simply wanted to find a way to tell others about Jesus Christ.

> *God loves you and has a wonderful plan for your life, as He had a plan for all mankind from the creation of the world. From Adam on, man has been separated from God by sin – "For all have sinned and fall short of the glory of God" (Rom. 3:23). In the Old Testament, men sacrificed animals to atone to God for their sins by the shedding of blood.*
>
> *Then, in His timing, God took action to bridge the gap between Himself and man. He came down to earth in the form of man – Jesus Christ. John 1:1 says, "In the beginning was the Word, and the Word was with God, and the Word was God." And John 1:14 says, "And the Word was made flesh and dwelt among us."*
>
> *Jesus lived, taught, and died on the cross so that the shedding of His blood would atone for our sins and bridge this gap between God and man. Jesus became sin for us. The penalty of man's sin was lifted by Jesus' resurrection from the dead.*
>
> *Each person must personally receive Jesus Christ as Savior and Lord to know and experience God's love and God's plan for his life.*

*   *   *

> *God has always been reaching out to man, trying to bring him back into a closer communion with Himself. After the fall of Adam, man was separated from God. Then Abraham came along, and God called him to follow. Abraham was called the "Father of the Faith" because he heard God and obeyed. Through him, God brought forth a race of people who were to be His special people of revelation. Later, when they were in bondage in Egypt, God called Moses to lead His people to freedom and back to the land He had promised them.*
>
> *Somehow, it seems that through the obedience of one of His own, God is always trying to reveal Himself. Moses was faithful, but a lot of the people grumbled and were ready to turn back to Egypt. This happened over and over again throughout the Old Testament. The people would fall away into sin and forget God. But God never forgot them – He was always calling them back to Himself through the prophets. And finally, in the fullness of time, He sent His Son Jesus to show to all people forever His divine love.*

Even then the people didn't understand, and they killed Him. God knew this would happen, but this is how great His love is for us. He sent His own Son (the Lamb of God) to be sacrificed for us – for all our sins. He died so that we might live and enjoy life abundantly. This is what God wants for us – that we might live abundantly, conscious of His love and presence with us as we live in His Son, our Lord Jesus.

This witness might be expressed in a drawing:

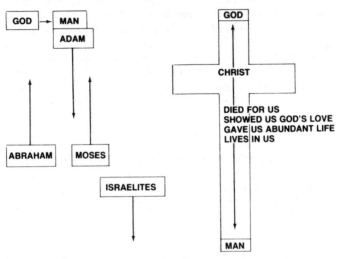

A witness could develop through a conversation in the following way:

"Joe, I've known you for a long time, and I don't think we've ever talked about religion, but I'd like to ask you a question: What do I do to become a Christian? What does it mean?"

"To become a Christian is a way of being free. It's a way of being free of many things that might bother you now. Christianity isn't giving up a lot of things, but it is getting something special. You don't really have to do much."

"I don't?"

"You don't have to attend a bunch of classes or study a whole lot of things to become a Christian. It's very simple, really, and that is why it is so difficult for many people – just the fact that it is so simple. All you have

46

to do is believe in Jesus Christ, that He is the Son of God, and that He loves you. He is waiting for you to accept Him now. He's always been waiting for you to accept Him. You just come to Him like a child. At our age, that's hard for some people to do."

"I don't know what you mean – to come to Him as a child."

"To come to Him just the same way you would go to your father, being submissive to Him and accepting what He says – believing in Him and that the things the Bible says about Him are true – believing that Jesus Christ is the Son of God, that He died for us, and that He lives for us right now. All you have to do is believe and ask Him to come into your life."

"That's all?"

"All you have to say is that you believe in Jesus Christ. Do you believe that Jesus Christ is the Son of God?"

"I would like to believe that."

"Is there any reason you would wonder about it? What would keep you from believing?"

"Well, I've always felt I wasn't quite good enough, that the things I've done weren't acceptable to Jesus."

"Well, I can tell you that no one is good enough, and I'm not either. But fortunately, God is like your father. You know, your father never said to you, 'You're not good enough to be my child.' He may have gotten upset with you at times, and he may have been hurt by some of the things you did, but he never said you were not his child. God is the same way. We do wrong, and continue to do wrong, but He just keeps on loving us. He loves us enough to accept us the way we are, the way we accept our own children when we say, 'I wish you wouldn't do things like that, but you're mine and I love you. You'll always be my child.' "

"He's ready to accept me just as I am?"

"That's right. If we had to wait until we were good enough, we'd all be waiting."

"You've answered lots of my questions, Joe, and I would like to accept Jesus."

Now is the time to seal the transaction by prayer and giving thanks together.

Sometimes our witnesses must be brief.

A clergyman in Portland, Oregon, was visiting a hospital when a nurse asked him if he had two or three minutes to spare. When he responded in the affirmative, she said, "Well, there's a man in here with a terminal illness

47

who probably has less than twenty-four hours to live. He doesn't have a single relative or friend in this town, and I'm concerned about him. Will you go in and see him?" The clergyman was then told that he could have only two or three minutes with the patient, so he went in as the nurse stood outside and watched.

"I'd like to talk to you about Jesus. Do you want to hear what I have to say?" the clergyman asked the dying man.

"Yes," came the reply.

"You know that you do not have much time left."

"Yes, I know."

"All right," the clergyman said, "if there was a doctor in this hospital who could come in here and take all the cancer out of your body and put it on his body and give you his perfect life, you would be well, wouldn't you?"

"Yes," replied the dying man, "but there's no such doctor."

"No, but that is what Jesus Christ did. He has taken all of your sin on Himself, and He gives you all of the forgiveness and cleansing that you need to meet God. Do you believe this?"

"Yes, I believe," the man replied.

Then the nurse said, "Time's up." The clergyman said a blessing over the man and left him in peace.

After reviewing the above witnesses and thinking about which portions of them are natural to us, we should write our witness on a piece of paper. Then, as we did with the testimony, we should present it to a Christian friend verbally and let him critique it. Following that, we should pray for the opportunity to give our witness to a non-Christian, that God may use us as an instrument through whom another person either accepts Jesus Christ as Lord and Savior or comes to see more clearly who Jesus Christ is, what He did, and why he should believe in Him.

A little prayer some people use is: "Dear Lord, here I am again, one of Your children. If You will open the way for me to witness to Your grace to someone in Your name, somehow I'll do it, by Your help."

Our witness will be of little value until we have prepared it and presented it in a real-life situation. If we are not willing to find a way in which we can naturally discuss with another who Jesus Christ is, we might as well close the book and not concern ourselves with the other ways in which we can show God's love. Willingness and obedience are at the heart of our obligation as Christians.

Study Assignment

1. Write out your witness.
2. Present it aloud (don't read it) to a Christian friend and let him critique it for you.
3. Pray that God will lead you to someone who needs to hear your witness.

Person No. 1

6 *The Prayer*

Person No. 1

6 *The Prayer*

Having shared a witness and testimony with Person No. 1, we now come to the point where he is ready to accept Jesus Christ as Lord and Savior. Our primary responsibility now is to lead him, through prayer, into such an acceptance.

As in other situations, there are several factors to take into consideration. First of all, it is quite likely that the individual has already "accepted" Christ; he simply will be going through the formality — although this is important — of making that profession in the presence of another. Further, this action on his part should be followed by the liturgical demonstration of this "acceptance" within the church of the individual's choosing by way of baptism, confirmation, etc.

If it is clear that he has already accepted Christ, we may want to take the simplest possible approach to expressing that acceptance in prayer. We may only need to say, "You have already accepted Christ, haven't you? Why don't we just thank Him for coming into your heart and taking over your life?" Otherwise, we may want to lead the individual through a more formal prayer of acceptance, using our own words.

There are several methods of handling the acceptance prayer. The best is to lead the individual to do the praying himself by pointing out to him that prayer is simply conversing with God and that God doesn't expect us to be able to do it in any special way. He knows us, loves us, and is willing to accept whatever we offer Him by way of prayer. If the individual then feels comfortable in proceeding to prayer, we should encourage him to do so. We may ask, "Why don't you say a prayer now?" Or, if we feel he needs more encouragement, we might say, "Would you put into words what you feel about Jesus Christ and about becoming a Christian? I'll be praying with you as you do." However, under no circumstances should we force him to pray if he is reluctant to do so.

Another method of praying is to lead the prayer in simple phrases and ask the individual to repeat them. We must be careful not to include in the prayer those things the individual would be reluctant to repeat. In other words, if he is accepting Christ out of a reaction to the bountiful goodness of God's love rather than out of a sense of extreme need to repent, we might lead him through a "loving acceptance" prayer rather than a "confession and repentance" prayer.

Finally, for the person who is extremely shy or otherwise greatly reluctant to do any praying, simply do the praying for him. Even here, however, we should tell the individual that we are going to say the prayer for him and that if he concurs with it, he should join us in saying "Amen" at the conclusion.

Having the above in mind, we now offer examples of acceptance prayers. These are not to be memorized for future use, but are simply to show that there are a variety of ways wherein the same thing can be accomplished.

1

Dear heavenly Father, we come to You now in thanksgiving that
_____ *is seeking to know You. I thank You so much that You can come into his heart and into his life, that You can come into his mind and give him the knowledge of Your presence with him right now. Open his ears and his eyes and his heart so that he may know and*

understand more clearly Your love for him, how much You care for him, and how much You have that You want to share with him. For we ask all of these things in the blessed name of Jesus Christ, our Lord. Amen.

2

Gracious holy Father, we thank You that _____ *has come to find Your Son, Jesus Christ, and to know Him, to know that He is with him in this and that He accepts him and loves him no matter what he does. We thank You, O Lord, and we pray that You will guide him and strengthen him in this wonderful walk with You. We offer our prayers in the name of that same Jesus Christ. Amen.*

3

Dear Jesus, I just want You. I need You. I open my heart and ask You to come in. You can come into all the dark corners of my life and do with me as You wish from now on, beginning right now. Thank You for doing that.

4

Thank You, Father, for accepting me just as I am. Thank You, Father.

5

Lord, I offer as much of myself as I can to as much of You as I understand. Amen.

Some people, for one reason or another, may not be willing to make a commitment at the end of our discussion with them. They need some time alone to think about what has been discussed. They may be like the person who had made many mental commitments through the years but had never committed his life to Jesus from his heart. He said, "I've done this sort of thing so many times. I've walked down so many aisles, and I just can't do it with you now." At that point, it is best to explain to the person, who is showing real honesty, that he can make his commitment to Jesus at any time and that no one else has to be around.

As with the other things we have learned, we should pray to have an opportunity to lead someone to Christ so we may be able to put into practice those principles we are learning, including how to pray with a person to receive Christ.

We have now finished a consideration of various factors that need to be taken into account in helping a person who has come to us with the desire of accepting Christ as Lord and Savior. We have outlined the basic things any individual needs to be prepared to do in helping those people who fall into the category of Person No. 1. All of these principles could also be applicable to any of the remaining six people with whom we may come into contact.

Study Assignment

1. Write out or act out how you would lead a person to pray to receive Christ once he is ready to do so.

2. Prepare a sample of a prayer you could use in encouraging a person to "repeat after me" his acceptance of Christ.

3. Prepare a sample of a prayer you might pray on behalf of another that he receive Christ.

Person No. 2

7 *One Who Shows an Interest*

Person No. 2

7 *One Who Shows an Interest*

Person No. 2 is the individual who expresses an interest in our lives as Christians, in Christ Himself, or in our church. We want to help him come to a decision about Christ, but we must work with him in a somewhat more delicate manner than with Person No. 1.

All of the principles we have considered in connection with Person No. 1 also apply to Person No. 2. However, there are other factors that need to be taken into consideration, the first being that Person No. 2 is not ready to accept Jesus Christ as his Savior. There is additional groundwork to be laid so that, if God has so prepared his heart, he will be ready to take that step.

If the person's interest is in the church or in our lives as Christians, we want to bring Jesus Christ into the conversation in a meaningful way. But we do not want to force this; we want the opportunity to develop naturally so that the mention of Jesus can be most effective.

We should be aware that there is power in the name of Jesus. In speaking to those who do not believe this, we should find ways to mention Jesus in particular situations relating to their lives, noting their reactions. Even in the apathetic world in which we live today, the name of Jesus does not evoke a casual response.

There is, of course, a reason for leading the person into a discussion about Jesus Christ. Despite the wonderful ways in which Christ may be working in our lives, we are not Christ, and we are not leading the person to accept us. One can become a Christian only by accepting Jesus Christ as his Savior.

Likewise, we are not interested in simply leading a person to accepting the church as an institution. We may have a wonderful church, but the church is not Christ Himself. There are many people who attend church for all the wrong reasons and have never come into a living relationship with Jesus Christ. Certainly it is better to lead a person into Christ's church as opposed to driving him off in some other direction, but our primary objective is to help the person see that what the church is about is Christ and that what he needs is a personal relationship with Jesus.

We should not forget that our discussion with Person No. 2 also involves a great deal of listening. We need to know where the individual is in his understanding of Christ and the extent to which he may be ready to know more. Again, this may be done by asking questions and turning questions so that the individual has an opportunity to develop his thoughts. In the course of this, he may want to know what Christ means in our lives, and that will give us an opportunity to give our testimony. However, we should be patient and wait for the right opportunity; we shouldn't force our testimony on a person before he is ready to hear it.

We should be able to identify with the person's needs, problems, and questions in an open and honest manner and provide him with a great quantity of loving acceptance. If we are aware of the opportunity to talk with this person about Christ before he actually comes to visit with us, that is our time to prepare with prayer. As we ask God to prepare our hearts to meet with Person No. 2, we can also ask Him to give us a genuine loving concern for the person so that he can see "something special" within us and in our attitude toward him as we talk about Christ. However, even if we have not had that opportunity to prepare, we should be praying within ourselves as we talk with Person No. 2. Where our walk toward the Lord parallels his, there is a point of special contact; as we have the opportunity to tell him of similar experiences we have had — without interfering with his train of thought or his presentation to us — we will help cement the relationship between us.

After Person No. 2 has given us a clear picture of where he is, we can then zero in on showing him, to the extent necessary, who Jesus Christ is and what He has done in our lives. Pay careful attention to what he says to determine whether he is getting the point and whether he is absorbing what we are saying.

We shouldn't argue with the individual. Rather, we should continue to show him that we love him even if there are points of serious disagreement. We should know that God has simply not prepared this person's heart to accept Christ at this time and not force the issue. On the other hand, if the "argument" is simply a search for understanding, we should patiently attempt to help him reach a proper understanding. Once we start losing our temper we will know we are arguing instead of gently explaining, and it is time to bring the discussion to a close.

On the other hand, if the discussion leads the person toward acceptance of Christ, we should be ready to react in the same positive manner as with Person No. 1. Talk with him about the matter of praying to receive Christ. Then urge him to do so or lead him in such a prayer.

If the discussion falls short of his accepting Christ as Savior, we shouldn't be discouraged. Whether Person No. 2 has become argumentative or is simply unready to take the step, we have still been an obedient servant of God's will, and we have sown seeds that will bear fruit later.

We must always leave the door open for further discussion, and we may do this by saying that we want to get more information for him and would like to set a date to meet again and discuss what we have found. We should always be ready to admit that we certainly do not "know everything," and our willingness to get further help from a Christian who may have answers to questions Person No. 2 has asked will strengthen our position in his eyes rather than indicating weakness on our part. He will probably be more comfortable with us if we don't "know it all."

If there is no further information to be obtained for Person No. 2, but we simply feel we can have a more productive conversation after he has had an opportunity to digest what has been said, we should let him know that we would like to get together again. We may just say, "I would like to talk with you further about this," and, if possible, set a date. That will force both of you to give the matter thought prior to the next discussion.

Study Assignment

By bringing Jesus Christ into a conversation in a meaningful way, we open the door for a Person No. 2 to reveal himself. That is, we give the person an opportunity to show that he has an interest in Christ.

Reconstruct one or more conversations you have had in the last week, and demonstrate how you brought — or could have brought — Jesus Christ into the conversation.

Person No. 3

8 *Our Uninterested Friend
or Relative*

Person No. 3

8 *Our Uninterested Friend or Relative*

Person No. 3 is our uninterested friend or relative. This is the individual who knows us well and yet shows no interest in Jesus Christ. He is apathetic about what is most important to us, and yet he is a person close to us through friendship or kinship. He is one of the most difficult tests we face as a Christian.

Before considering the various factors involved in trying to share God's love with Person No. 3, it would probably be fruitful to consider a number of the reasons why we are likely to have so much difficulty with him.

1. *Person No. 3 simply knows us too well.* He sees our imperfections, our worst characteristics as well as our best. He might be the one who told us when we were in the fifth grade that we were dumb and he never expected us to have much sense; now that we are Christian, he believes that is proof of our ignorance or is some fad we are pursuing.

Perhaps if Person No. 3 is a relative, we have had serious difficulty with him in the past. There may have been a family dispute as a result of an inheritance (one of the most divisive issues families face). We may not have been committed to Christ at the time the dispute arose, and the members of our

65

family who were on the other side of the dispute may find it extremely difficult to believe we have changed.

Likewise, many of our friends know what we are like in both our "B.C." and "A.D." states. What they knew of us before we met Christ cannot be erased from their minds. They often can see only the "carry-over traits" and not the ways in which we have changed for the better (for instance, if those changes are negative to their life style, they choose to ignore them). With Person No. 3, we often have a "familiarity breeds contempt" problem.

2. *Perhaps we want too badly to share Christ with Person No. 3 and thus find it difficult to be objective with him.* Because he is our friend or relative, we may feel a special calling to lead him into the relationship with Jesus Christ that now means so much to us, and our intensity scares Person No. 3. However, because we are so close to him, we cannot move any discussion of Jesus Christ into an objective situation where it can be dealt with rationally. Thus we tend to become too tense and bring too much of our own "garbage" into the issue. We wind up by turning him off.

On the other hand, Person No. 3's resistance may be just plain stubbornness. The more diligently someone tries to get us to change, the more we tend to dig in our heels and say, "I don't have to do that just because you did it." We can expect Person No. 3 to react to us in the same way if we are too intense in trying to share Christ with him.

3. *To Person No. 3 we are a "prophet without honor."* Jesus had that problem Himself. Whether because of jealousy or other factors, the people who know us best are the ones least likely to accept what we have to offer that is strange to them.

4. *The very closeness of the relationship between us and Person No. 3 makes any change in our lives threatening to him.* There is the story of the man who went to church regularly with his wife, seemed to enjoy the service, the sermon, the fellowship, and the singing, but consistently refused to become a Christian until he was on his deathbed. When someone asked him why, he said, "Well, I would have had to pray like my wife." There was something

there in the closeness of that relationship that threatened him to the core.

5. *In addition to being threatening to Person No. 3, it can be threatening to us to share Christ with him.* If we talk to someone close to us about Christ, we fear that we may never be able to talk about anything to him again — he may simply cut us off. We would rather retain the status quo than alienate him completely.

6. *There is nothing specifically Christian about loving Person No. 3.* One of the most effective ways of bringing people into a personal relationship with Jesus Christ is the fact that we love them and are concerned about them even though they are not friends or relatives. When the individual is, however, a Person No. 3, there is nothing special about our showing him our love and concern. He feels he is due that anyway. Therefore, one of the most effective means of sharing God's love is of little use to us.

7. *It may be that our new life in Christ is not in accordance with the plan that Person No. 3 had for us.* He is experiencing disappointment with what is happening in our lives. Our friend or loved one can see that we are living by a different set of standards from the ones he is accustomed to, and he can see no reason why he should change just because we have. Yet, if he is to remain close to us, what is he to do but resent the change in us? Our parents may have had a special plan for our lives, and now we are living for Christ instead of in accordance with their plans.

8. *Finally, it is quite possible that, over the years, we have never talked about Jesus Christ with Person No. 3, and that very absence of discussion now stands as a barrier to our doing so.*

These are only a few of the many problems looming ahead as we try to share God's love with Person No. 3. The intent here is not to begin with a negative approach, but simply to be realistic about the obstacles facing us. With those obstacles in mind, we will be better able to determine the extent to which we can share God's love with Person No. 3, and by this set our goals more realistically.

As we will see, there are many ways to share God's love other than giving our testimony or witness. The difficulties in discussing Christ with Person No. 3 should simply give us more incentive to use these alternate methods in hopes that, through them, either we or someone else will ultimately be able to lead him into a living relationship with Jesus Christ.

Study Assignment

Make a list of three or four persons who fit into the category of Person No. 3. Under the name of each, list everything you can think of (from this chapter and otherwise) that might make it difficult for you to share God's love with him.

Person No. 3

9 *What We Can Do*

9 *What We Can Do*

Now that we have considered reasons why it is difficult to share God's love with the uninterested friend or relative, let us explore what we *can* do.

1. *First, we should question whether our life styles have changed since we accepted Christ, and whether the new life styles are changing continually as we are molded into Christ's image.* Although, as noted in the prior chapter, the very changing of our lives can create a problem for Person No. 3, our failure to change in the manner Christ calls us to change is hypocritical. We have to allow the change to take place, regardless of the consequences. God can redeem the problems created by our obedience to Him.

Moreover, our failure to be conformed to the desires of Christ represents a negative witness not only to Person No. 3, but to all others with whom we come into contact. Here, of course, we are not talking about artificial changes of life style (the adoption of unloving rules and regulations that we impose on ourselves and others), but the natural change in values that should occur in our lives when Jesus Christ is our priority. Do our lives — our basic actions and reactions — show that Christ is the most important factor in our existence? If not, we have some soul-searching ahead of us as we prayerfully adjust to that plan of life to which He calls us. We can expect to have no positive effect on Person No. 3 until Christ has had an effect on us.

Our lives should show consistency in moving in the direction Christ leads us. Flourishes of activity in one direction followed by disobedience and depression in the other will not be a good witness to the individual who knows us intimately, and Person No. 3 is the one who knows us best. Again, if there is not a pattern of constructive growth as we have begun to follow Christ, self-examination is in order. In fact, it will be extremely difficult for us to try to lead Person No. 3 toward Christ unless we have gotten our own lives on the right track. We do not mean that we, as Christians, must attain a state of sinlessness before we seek to help others. What we are saying is that we are always witnesses — for good or for bad — and have an obligation to keep our own lives in order as we proceed to show God's love to others.

2. *Because he is uninterested, Person No. 3 needs to experience a supernatural revelation of God's love.* We need to pray for a supernatural event that will awaken him to the fact that Jesus Christ is alive in the world today. It will be through such an awakening that we are given an opportunity to share God's love with him in a way that would be entirely ineffective unless he has seen this new dimension in his life.

Further, we can pray that *we* will experience a supernatural revelation that will be meaningful to Person No. 3. An example is the Christian who while in church with his brother was overcome with tears of joy. There was no way to explain the tears to the brother (the typical Person No. 3) in a rational manner, yet the brother knew that the experience was real. It opened him up to be led to the Lord in a way that neither person would have expected unless the Christian had been praying for a supernatural event.

3. *Likewise, a crisis in the life of a Person No. 3 can be the circumstance through which we are able to share God's love most effectively with him.* We are not suggesting prayer for such crises to occur in the lives of our uninterested friends and relatives. However, we

should pray to be prepared when Person No. 3 does experience a death in the family, an illness or hospitalization, loss of his job, a disastrous financial setback, or some serious family problem. Knowing that such crises do occur in everyone's life, we can wait for it to happen in the life of Person No. 3 and be ready to help him in his need.

The more severe the crisis, the more possible it is for Christ to reach people through it. One family, who had consistently ignored the attempts of a Christian friend to share Christ with them, completely changed when the husband was killed in an accident. Almost immediately, the wife and children accepted Christ and came into loving fellowship with the church which ministered to their special needs.

Often people must be brought to a serious illness before they can see that they do not have control of their lives and must seek help from a Christian friend or relative. One Christian simply gave her cross to a loved one to hold during the night before a cancer operation as assurance of the presence of God with her. The next morning, still clutching the cross, this Person No. 3 prayed to receive Christ and went into major surgery with Christ's joy written all over her face.

Friends and relatives who seem to totally ignore our interest in Christ will often ask us to pray for them as they face a crisis, and that opening can lead into a witness through which they come into a living relationship with Jesus. Again, the important thing is to be prepared. We should maintain such a closeness of contact with them that we know the crises they face, and we should pray to have the compassion through which they can see God's love in us. That combination of factors is ideal if we are to serve God in bringing our friends and relatives into His fold.

4. *Sensitivity to needs is the key to being effective in the situations set forth in the above paragraphs.* If Person No. 3 is truly a friend or a close relative, it is common to assume we will automatically be sensitive to his needs. However, it is only as we allow the love of God to flow through us that we can have the sensitivity necessary to deal with crises and supernatural revelations in the most

effective manner. That sensitivity involves much prayer. If we are to be witnesses to Christ, we must do hard work "on our knees" that He may speak to us about what is happening in the lives of others and how we may be instruments of His mercy and grace in bringing His healing love to those situations.

5. *As we look for opportunities to share God's love with Person No. 3, we need to pray that God will empty us of ourselves.* In the previous chapter, we discussed the problem of our relationship with Person No. 3 as being too subjective, our wanting too badly to bring him to Christ, and the intensity of the relationship that thereby exists. These factors may be overcome only to the extent that we can get ourselves out of the picture and let God's Holy Spirit work through us. Emily Gardiner Neal, the well-known author in the healing ministry, prays that God will use her to minister to every person with whom she comes into contact. However, she precedes this with a prayer that God will empty her of herself so that He can do the work. She prays that she will not get in the way.

Left to ourselves, we tend to want to manipulate situations with Person No. 3. If we are unable to reach our friend or relative with the saving message of Christ, we often want to arrange to get him alone with someone else who can perhaps carry out this purpose. We must be careful to let God arrange such encounters and not engineer them ourselves.

Further, we must deal with our own self-righteousness. If our Christianity comes across as being narrow, blind, or falsely pious, we can drive him away from the Lord. To avoid this eventuality, we need to remind ourselves that evangelism is "one beggar telling another beggar where to find bread."

6. *We should sow seeds of God's love whenever we have opportunity.* Bringing a person to the Lord is often a slow, heart-melting process, and this is especially true with someone like Person No. 3. In effect, his heart is cold to what we have to share. To help him see that God does love him and is present to help him in everyday situations of life can be as difficult as melting an iceberg.

Person No. 3 – What We Can Do

One of the best ways to sow seeds is to share with Person No. 3, in a natural, conversational way, some of the things we know are happening in the lives of others. We should avoid confronting our friend or relative by asking questions or directly applying to him the experiences of other people. However, simply telling stories of people's experiences with God in all aspects of life, matter-of-factly but almost casually, can have a melting effect. Many people who would have fought any attempt at confrontation have become Christians because someone close to them loved them enough to expose them constantly, yet unthreateningly, to what God is doing.

Obviously, the seeds of God's love can be sown in many other ways. Continuing kindnesses "above and beyond the call of duty" will make even a close friend or relative ultimately wonder, *Why is he doing this for me?* If, in fact, we are not doing it for any selfish purpose, but only because we allow God's love to flow through us, we have cultivated the garden wherein our "seeds" can come to fruition. Those same seeds are sown by the example we set in the life we live, by the way in which we give God the credit for the gracious goodness we receive, by the strength of character we manifest in the crucial decisions we must make, and by the myriad other opportunities to live in accordance with God's plan which cannot be ignored by our friends and relatives.

7. *Recognize that there are difficulties in sharing Christ with Person No. 3,* as we discussed in detail in the last chapter. Discover those specific difficulties that may be creating problems in talking with the particular Person No. 3. Then pray not only for discernment of the difficulties, but for sensitivity to the special ways in which God can help resolve them. Although God will give us abundant help, He does expect us to figure out some things for ourselves!

Because we have been close to Person No. 3, perhaps for many years, it is quite possible we have wronged him in the past and have never sought forgiveness. This, of course, is a wonderful opportunity to reflect God's love. If we can be concerned enough about Person No. 3 to have probed our lives and found those areas wherein we have, through action or inaction, treated him unfairly (being careful to consider only real offenses and not contriving something so we can use forgiveness as a technique), and if we can truly ask for forgiveness, we can reflect Christ in all His glory. The readiness to humble oneself before another is one of the clearest marks of a Christian. Chances are that even Person No. 3 can see that.

8. *As we have prayed that God will reveal to us the specific difficulties we face in sharing Christ with Person No. 3, we may also pray to discover the particular roadblock our friend or relative has encountered in accepting Christ.* We can then pray for guidance concerning that roadblock and wait for the God-given opportunity to knock it down. If we do this in a gentle and loving way, Person No. 3 may come into his own personal walk with our Lord. When we get specific about our prayers, it is amazing how we receive the special guidance we need to help the person whom God would have us love.

9. *We need to pray for an encircling of God's love, not only around Person No. 3, but around ourselves when we are with him.* If we have feelings of resentment toward Person No. 3, we should quietly and prayerfully work through that until our hearts are filled with overflowing love for him. Then, when we are next in his company, all that we project will be positive and constructive, and the groundwork will be laid toward leading him a step closer to Christ. If, on the other hand, we project bitterness, frustration, or hopelessness, we may drive Person No. 3 further from the goal we seek.

There are many other opportunities to study the difficulties that interfere with our sharing Christ with this person. But if we are willing, prayerfully and creatively, to seek to overcome those difficulties that Christ may be made manifest, we can make progress in our witness.

10. *In dealing with Person No. 3, we must be careful not to answer questions which are not being asked.* Keep in mind that the lack of interest on the part of our friend or relative means he does not

want us to preach to him. If we intentionally misinterpret the questions he does ask in order to give him answers that we want to impose upon him, we have once again allowed ourselves to get into a manipulative position. Instead, we should follow our Lord's leading and wait for Him to create those situations and circumstances in which Person No. 3 will ask the "right" questions — those we can properly answer in such a manner that Jesus Christ will be glorified.

11. *Patience and trust must be at the foundation of our continued relationship with Person No. 3.* We must trust that God will move in him in His own time. If we can have faith that the problem of Person No. 3 is really one that only God can solve, we can have the patience to wait for God to work it out.

12. *Finally, we should show consistent love and concern for our uninterested friend or relative, while at the same time avoiding any hint of coercion in dealing with him.* We should never cease praying for him. Nor should we fail to take advantage of any of the above — or other — opportunities that may exist to make Christ known to him. Remember the story of Monica who prayed for so many years that her hell-raising son would ultimately come to the Lord; and through the years, that son, Saint Augustine, has stood out as a preeminent Christian witness.

We have now considered many factors that apply to sharing God's love with our uninterested friend or relative. We have seen that, despite the multitude of difficulties we face in dealing with such a person, God gives us many opportunities to show forth His love. Some of us will have the unparalleled blessing of leading a Person No. 3 to accept Jesus Christ as his Savior, and all of us will have continuing occasions to sow seeds that will lead to that harvest.

Study Assignment

Choose two of the persons you listed as a part of your assignment for chapter 8 and develop a plan for sharing God's love with each of them, leaving plenty of room for God to guide you through His Holy Spirit.

Person No. 4

10 Our Uninterested Neighbor

Person No. 4

10 *Our Uninterested Neighbor*

Slightly different from our uninterested friend or relative is Person No. 4: our uninterested neighbor. This is the person who may not know us intimately — for better or worse — but who does know how we live. There are certainly similarities between trying to share Christ with him and with Person No. 3; therefore, virtually all the possibilities we have considered in the previous chapter apply here.

However, a number of special opportunities suggest themselves as we attempt to show forth Christ to Person No. 4.

1. *We can invite Person No. 4 into our lives.* He has not become a friend (in the sense of Person No. 3), so he probably does not know much about our commitment to Jesus Christ. Until he has the opportunity to know us better, our chances to share Christ with him aren't much different from those we have with someone we simply come into contact with on the street. As we bring him into our lives, he can see how Christ affects us in ways that should be constructively revealing to him.

Of course, the more contact we have with Person No. 4, as a result of inviting him into our lives, the more opportunity we have to tell him about Christ. We can initiate this in a multitude of ways, not the least of which is simply availing ourselves of opportunities to visit with him. From there we can move into the realm of social contact by inviting him and his family to dinner or to participate in any other type of general family project that might be of interest to them. Such projects do not have to be "religious" in nature, but are simply means by which Person No. 4 can get to know us better. Here we have the specific opportunity to do what God calls us to do — that is, to love our neighbor.

It is, of course, all right to let our neighbors know we are going to church when they casually ask us where we are going. However, as the occasion presents itself, we really should tell them why we go to church so often and what is happening there. When we talk vaguely about the church and all the work we do there, but fail to reveal the significance of the church, we are not challenging a person to give his life to Jesus Christ.

2. *There is something lovable about our neighbor.* While recognizing that his physical proximity to us has shown him our faults, we have probably noticed some of his. If we dwell on our neighbor's faults, we will tend to build up walls of resistance between him and ourselves. Instead, we need to find something lovable about our neighbor and focus on that. As we allow God to show us his good points, we build a love for him that is affirmative and paves the way for sharing God's love with him.

3. *We should avail ourselves of the opportunity not only to "do favors" for our neighbor, but to let him do things for us.* As we allow the growth of a mutual reliance and interdependence, we are laying a foundation on which a true friendship can exist. If Christ is a part of that friendship from the first, we do not run into as many difficulties as with Person No. 3 (who was probably our friend before Christ became the center of our lives). Because Christ is a part of us, He becomes a part of the friendship and a part of that mutual reliance and interdependence. Our neighbor comes to see that we are more than just a neighbor and friend — we are someone who can deal with special problems in a special way because God is our guide.

4. *As our neighbor begins to share his life with us, we should be open to hearing his problems.* As with others with whom we have an opportunity to share Christ, we should have a listening ministry. It is as Person No. 4 tells us about his life, his interests, and his concerns that we can see where he is in his attitude toward Christ.

By listening to his problems, we can help him find proper solutions. Many times solutions will involve routine and earthly matters. Eventually, however, as we show our love over a period of time, we may be able to share with our neighbor the ultimate answer to all of his problems.

5. *We must convey the message, "God loves you."* A good time to tell our neighbor that God loves him is when he is sharing his problems with us. An easy approach is to hear him out and then say, "Well, you talk as though God is dead." He may reply, "I think He is!" Here is the occasion for us to say, "Have I got good news for you! God loves you!" If we have "done our homework" in this book thus far, we should know how to carry the conversation from there toward leading Person No. 4 at least one step closer to Christ, if not into a full relationship with Him at that moment.

6. *Neighborhoods are often centers of controversy; living close to other people is not easy.* Controversies we have with Person No. 4 are unique occasions for showing God's love. The opportunity is similar to the one we have in asking a Person No. 3 for forgiveness. The humility we should be learning from Christ allows us to surrender our rights for the benefit of our neighbor. Our neighbor may feel that our children make too much noise or that they are hard on his lawn, but he can overlook such small matters if, in something that seems major to him, we are willing to "go the second mile" because the love of Christ in us allows us to do so. That is something our neighbor will take notice of and it will create an attitude in his heart that will prepare for a presentation of Christ.

7. *Something less dramatic but often effective is the possibility of a book or cassette ministry to Person No. 4.* Here we share with him the

things we have read and heard which have been helpful to us and we feel will be of interest to him. People like being given or loaned a book or cassette, and that creates a receptivity to the very message contained therein. Obviously, we should be careful in the selection of material we give to our neighbor; if we present him with something too far removed from his present mode of thinking, we will simply create a credibility gap. Here, again, sensitivity is the key.

8. *Likewise, we have an excellent opportunity with our neighbor for "secondary evangelism."* "Secondary evangelism" simply means inviting our neighbor into situations whereby others may help him come to know the Lord. It may involve inviting him to come to church with us or asking him to participate in some other Christian activity if he is not ready to accompany us to a regular worship service. Visiting speakers, church picnics, and other activities provide unique opportunities to invite our neighbor to learn who Jesus Christ is. Here again, sensitivity should be used; if we try to move Person No. 4 too far too fast, we may "scare him off." We should seek the Lord's guidance and His timing in using secondary evangelism with our neighbor.

9. *Perhaps the most crucial area of consideration in sharing God's love with our neighbor is our decision to follow through with him toward, into, and through his walk with the Lord.* Little progress is made in bringing a person to accept Christ unless we are also willing to help him combat the normal problems faced by the new Christian and nurture him within the loving fellowship of the church. It is a sacrifice of time on our part to become so involved with our neighbor, but it is exactly that kind of sacrifice to which our Lord calls us.

Our neighbor may not be the easiest person to lead to Christ. However, as can be seen from the above discussion, there are many opportunities to move him in that direction. If we set about the job armed with these ideas and God's love, we will surely reap some fruit.

When we do, our obligation to our neighbor has just begun.

We do not lead our neighbor to Christ and then say, "Whew! I did it! Now I can think about somebody else." Instead, we will simply have increased our involvement with our neighbor and our obligation to him. And we will have gained a brother.

Study Assignment

Prayerfully develop a plan to share God's love with a neighbor with whom you have had little contact.

Person No. 5

11 One With Whom We Come Into Contact

Person No. 5

11 *One With Whom We Come Into Contact*

Person No. 5 is the person with whom we come into contact daily — or he may be someone we meet only once. We may work with him, or we may see him regularly as we go about the routine of our daily life. On the other hand, he may be a person we have never seen before. We may sit beside him on an airplane flight, or some similar one-time exposure may place us close together.

As in other instances, there are a number of factors peculiar to our relationship with Person No. 5. He knows virtually nothing about us nor we about him. As we may be limited in the amount of time we are able to spend with him, there may be no opportunity for him to become a friend on a continuing basis. Yet God has brought us together, and that means we will be able to show God's love if we are really willing to do so.

When we are talking with a stranger and we know we will have a limited time together, we can afford to be a little stronger in our approach than we normally would. That helps us get right to the heart of the matter.

There are several things we should consider using as God's opportunities in our contacts with Person No. 5.

1. *First of all, we should consider the external signs through which we might bring Person No. 5 immediately into a conversation where either a witness or a testimony can be given.* Today, more and more Christians are wearing crosses and other symbols of their faith around their necks and on their lapels. This should not be done lightly, for we should expect that others will ask us about the significance of such signs and symbols, and we should be ready to speak easily about our faith in Christ.

Further, if we are going to wear jewelry identifying ourselves as Christians, we should wear it as Christians. What is a worse witness than a person with a cross around his neck taking the Lord's name in vain? Obviously, the jewelry we wear should be modest and appropriate.

Finally, we should wear our Christian signs and symbols as outward expressions of an inner desire to share God's love. Many people have worn crosses without having any desire to share Christ, and they have found that people never ask them about their crosses. Others have prayed that their crosses would be the occasion for another person to inquire about Christ, and they have found frequent opportunities to witness. Such signs and symbols can truly be ideal "icebreakers" with which to begin meaningful conversations with a Person No. 5.

2. *Carrying a Bible or a devotional book can also be significant for the person with whom we come into contact.* However, such books should *not* be carried just for the sake of attracting attention. If our primary interest is in Christ, it is quite possible we will have a Bible or devotional book with us on a trip, in a waiting room, or in similar situations. When that is the natural and proper thing, it, too, can serve as an excellent "icebreaker." The precautions and preparations mentioned under the previous section apply here.

3. *If we are Christians, it is natural for us to be discussing various facets of our life in Christ.* Christian conversation can also be the means whereby we attract Person No. 5. The infectiousness of what we say, particularly if we are dealing with the experiences of the Christian life or mentioning the name of Jesus, can evoke

both positive and negative reactions from those around us. Whether or not the reaction is positive, it can be a real opportunity for us to share God's love.

4. *Warm, personal interest in the reason for a person's trip or his business can lead us into genuine contact with Person No. 5.* Such conversation may be all another individual will need in order for us to mention the name of Christ in a meaningful way. If we are willing to be God's instrument, we will welcome these opportunities and be prepared to use them effectively, applying principles we have already learned in this book and elsewhere in our walk with Christ.

5. *We may, of course, pray to be led to the prepared heart, the Person No. 5 who is ready to accept Jesus Christ as His Lord and Savior, if we are willing to be available for that purpose.* Ros Rinker shared this with us: "When I pray such a prayer, I have many opportunities to tell people about Jesus Christ. It is a prayer God will honor over and over again if we ask it from our hearts. I pray that God will lead me to that person who is prepared by Him to receive Christ, and then leave both the preparation and the results to Him."

6. *Obviously, with any Person No. 5 we have the opportunity to sow the seeds of God's love.* As we have studied earlier, we can do it by talking of the experiences of the Christian life that we and others have had; we can show it by actions of love and concern which God puts within us; and we can manifest it through the "otherness" that should be evident in our lives as we are submitted to God for guidance according to His plan. Keith Miller tells a story on this point in *A Second Touch:*

> *Several years ago a very busy business executive in an eastern city was rushing to catch a train. He had about given up trying to live a "personal" daily life because of the great demands on his time – speaking engagements and administrative duties in his organization. This particular morning en route to Grand Central Station he promised himself that he would try to be a Christian that day instead of only talking about it. By the time he had picked up his ticket, he was late. Charging across the lobby with his bags and down the ramp, he heard the last "all aboard." He was about to get on*

*the train when he bumped into a small child with his suitcase. The little boy
had been carrying a new jigsaw puzzle, the pieces of which were now
scattered all over the platform.*

*The executive paused, saw the child in tears, and with an inward sigh,
stopped, smiled, and helped the boy pick up his puzzle, as the train pulled
out.*

*The child watched him intently. When they finished picking up all of the
pieces, the little boy looked at the man with a kind of awe. "Mr.," he said
hesitantly, "are you Jesus?"*

*And for the moment the man realized that — on that platform — he had
been.* [1]

The Lord can guide us in all sorts of ways in sharing His love
with others. Here is one person's example.

*I was in church one day and noticed the woman in the pew in front of me
beginning to sob. I could tell she was really suffering. I reached over and
said, "Remember, you're never alone. He promised He would never leave
you or forsake you." I found out later that this woman's husband had been
killed a short time before and that she had never gotten over it. I didn't
know that, nor did I know who she was at the time, but I felt the Lord
leading me simply to give her a gentle touch.*

Those seeds of God's love may just be a part of a process
which leads Person No. 5 to Christ many years later, but it also
may be an opportunity for him to begin to ask us those questions which reveal where he is and provide us with the occasion
to testify or witness to Christ. We may even be allowed the
privilege of leading Person No. 5 to understand how near he is
to an acceptance of Jesus Christ as Lord and Savior.

7. *Of course, our contact with Person No. 5 gives us another excellent
opportunity for a listening ministry.* Our very willingness to hear his
problems or to help him make a decision he faces shows that
God's love flows through us. After we have done a great deal of
listening, the possibility always exists that we will have occasion to tell him how much God loves him, and, through that, to
lead him toward an acknowledged faith in Jesus Christ.

8. *There are opportunities to show God's love to Person No. 5 even
though we never come into speaking contact with him.* We have the

opportunity to love people all day long through our eyes, our smiles, and our spirits if we have prepared ourselves, through prayer, for Christ's love to flow through us. This is God's world, and anything we do to show His love draws people closer to Him, whether or not they know that the one who smiles at them is a Christian. It simply "makes them feel good." And the more God can "make people feel good" through instruments of His love, the sooner such people will come to accept Jesus Christ. We should simply pray that God will fill our hearts with peace, joy, and love that will reflect themselves through us in an infectious way to those we are privileged to see during the course of the day; then God will use us to His great purpose and to our great satisfaction.

9. *Finally, there is a wonderful opportunity to pray for those around us, asking God to meet their special needs.* Often when we've been in a waiting room or restaurant and have done this we've noticed that, in doing so, others will look up at us and smile. Nothing more may result than that passing of God's love. However, times will come when such people will get up, come over, and start a conversation with us and give us the opportunity to witness to them.

Although our contacts with Person No. 5 may involve less opportunity to share God's love because they are fleeting and uninvolved, we will probably come into contact with more people of this category than any other. Therefore, we can profit considerably from a thorough understanding of all the opportunities to share God's love with the thousands of strangers (many of whom, through Christ, will become brothers) we will meet in the days and years ahead.

Keith Miller tells another story about a Person No. 5 in *A Second Touch:*

> On the way to work I stopped for gasoline at the service station I had been patronizing for several years. The attendant smiled and said, "Good morning, Mr. Miller." I was sort of shocked as I realized that I had seen this man dozens of times and yet had never really noticed him as a person.

He knew my name, and I didn't have the vaguest idea what his was. And I was the Christian witness. I saw that this man was a person to whom God had introduced me to love for Him. Glancing quickly at the name tag on his uniform, I said, "Good morning, Charlie." After he had serviced the car and I was signing the credit card receipt, I tried to think of some natural thing to say to a man whom I had ignored for three years to let him know that I was interested in him as a person. Because suddenly I was. I finally came out with, "Say, Charlie, do you have a family?"

He stopped and looked at me a second. When he saw that I really seemed to want to know, his smile spread clear across his face. "Do I have a family?" And he pulled out his wallet with pictures of "about" nine children. This was the beginning of a new relationship which soon became a first name friendship with Charlie. One of his kids later got seriously injured in an accident. When I read about it in the paper, I knew who it was and could go and find out what might be done, not as a "Christmas-basket Christian," but as a friend – because we were already friends at the station. [2]

Study Assignment

Write out or act out two recent situations in which you were in contact with a Person No. 5 and show what you would now do as a result of what you have learned in chapter 11.

[1] Keith Miller, *A Second Touch* (Waco, Texas: Word Books, 1967) pp. 63, 64.
[2] Ibid., p. 58.

Person No. 6

12 *One Who Opposes What We Believe*

Person No. 6

12   *One Who Opposes*
What We Believe

We now consider the person who opposes what we believe as a Christian and who, in one way or another, lets us know it. He may unleash a verbal attack privately or in a public place, or he may simply fume when he is around us, particularly if we are saying anything about what Christ means to us. By these and other actions, this person seeks to make it clear to us that our love for Jesus Christ is a source of irritation to him.

Before discussing the particular factors we need to consider in our relationships with Person No. 6, we should recognize that this person is more likely to be led to an acceptance of Christ than the person who is apathetic. Person No. 6 knows he has a need (whether he admits it openly or not), but he is presently not considering Christ as the answer to that need. His reason is probably that he has had some bad experience with a Christian or with what he thought was Christianity. Our primary purpose, then, is to get to the bottom of his problem that we may be able to lead him toward the Answer. A "case history" might be helpful at this point:

> *Once I was in a gas station having tires put on the car and saw a fellow standing over at the side holding his index finger up as though he were*

pointing at the sky. I felt that the Lord was asking me to talk with him, so I asked him what he was doing. He said he was trying to see which direction the wind was blowing from because he was getting ready to have a smoke. He then went on to say what a terrible time he was having in trying to give up smoking. I told him that I had some friends who had asked the Lord to help them give up smoking, and He did. Then the fellow said, "Well, that's all right if you have a lot of faith." So I asked him if he was a Christian, and he said that he had been raised in the church, but that he could not accept the fact that Jesus was God. "I think the church is just perpetuating something for itself." He didn't mean that, and over the next two or three months he came to accept Jesus Christ as his Lord and Savior. In many cases, a fellow who opposes you is really asking for something.

Some things to consider in our contacts with Person No. 6 are:

1. *We must avoid arguments.* Any argument we get into with Person No. 6 simply puts his problem on the lowest possible level and a long way from Jesus Christ. Argument separates, and this person is already suffering from a great enough separation. Refrain from any further agitation which could bluntly challenge the things he might say.

2. *Again, listening is in order,* because we need to know what it is that Person No. 6 opposes, what happened in his past that created the problem, who wronged him, or what the problem may be. He has some reason for feeling the way he does, and when he realizes that, he is much more likely to come out with it. Our job, then, is to listen carefully, ask him questions in a loving manner, and "turn his questions" so he may develop his point of view.

3. *We need to love Person No. 6 as he talks with us rather than building up resentment toward him or becoming busy trying to think of answers to what he is saying.* Scripture promises us that God's Holy Spirit will give us the answers we need. Now is not the time to be clever or to attempt to outsmart Person No. 6. All we should do is listen and love until he has exhausted his fury and has made it clear to us "where he is." Then, if we have prepared ourselves and are open to the Lord's guidance, He will gently lead us into what we are to say and do.

4. If Person No. 6 has occasion to be around us from time to time, *we can expect him to insult us or rudely ignore us.* If we can keep in perspective the fact that he has a problem and needs God's love, we can see these incidents as opportunities leading toward a helpful confrontation for him and a glorious opportunity for us.

5. *Additionally, we should never take Person No. 6's attitude personally.* Whether or not he knows it, he is attacking Christ, not us. He can't see Christ, but he can see us, so he is going to attack the most tangible thing available to him that represents Christ. If we realize this, we can be assured that Christ can carry this burden for us. Keep in mind that we are involved in a spiritual battle and not a battle between earthly personalities. We should pray for help in maintaining objectivity in this regard while being subjective in our concern for the individual attacking us.

6. *In all events, we must keep calm!* Whether or not we get into an argument with Person No. 6, if our reaction is one of hostility he will sense it and will not be helped. However, if we can absorb his hostility without reacting, we are showing him something about God's love which can help him. While under attack by Person No. 6, we should constantly pray that God's Holy Spirit will keep us calm.

7. *We need not defend God.* He can take care of Himself. William H. Folwell, the Episcopal Bishop of Central Florida, testifies that he trudged through his own "dark night of the soul" during which he used his wits to try to convince people of the authenticity of Christ. It was only as he fell into despair concerning the situation that he was able to hear God tell him, "I never asked you to defend Me, only to proclaim Me." Intellectual defense of Christ only comes across as argument and is ultimately unproductive.

8. *Further, we should not avoid encounters with Person No. 6.* Every encounter is an opportunity to show God's love, even if we simply absorb punishment. It may take many such encounters before the individual will be willing to share enough of himself

with us so that we can be helpful to him in a specific way. If we avoid encounters, we are simply telling God that we are not available for Him to use in leading this person to Christ. Obviously, however, if we have not matured in our own relationship with Christ sufficiently to withstand such abuse, this particular point would not apply to us. Rather, we would need to seek guidance that we might become more mature.

9. *As the opportunity presents itself, however, we should sow as many "God loves you" seeds as we are able.* Again, we should not do it in an argumentative manner, but as reassurance to the tortured person with whom we are dealing. He desperately needs to know that fact, and he cannot be healed until we are able to convey it in some manner.

10. *As we have an opportunity to speak, it is extremely important to remember that, although we have the ultimate Answer, we do not have "all the answers."* We must be willing to admit that there are things we do not understand about our relationship with Christ, either in regard to the problems of everyday life or apparent contradictions within the Bible. If Person No. 6 throws too many questions at us, we should simply say (as Ros Rinker does), "Those are very good questions. I certainly don't have answers for all of them, but Christ has more answers for me than anything else. I have a lot of questions of my own. I'm working on some I have right now, but I get enough answers to satisfy my heart and to know that God loves me. That gives me security because I know that He is with me and I'm not on my own."

Person No. 6 will probably respect us for our honesty in admitting we don't have all the answers, whereas he will resent us if we simply throw him pat answers to his questions. Again, this is an area in which God's Holy Spirit will give us guidance if we will simply be prayerful in our relationship with Person No. 6.

11. *If the opportunity presents itself, it might be appropriate to ask this person if he has read the New Testament (or the Gospels) in a modern translation.* We often find that people who oppose Christ and are

confused have a garbled understanding of the Bible which they were taught years ago. Since they became adults, few have actually read the New Testament in one of the many modern translations available today. We should encourage Person No. 6 to do so.

12. *Despite all we have said about avoiding argument, we should express our belief in Christ to Person No. 6 as we have an opportunity to do so, so that he knows he has not talked us out of our position.* We do not need to preach to him; we simply need to affirm the fact that Jesus Christ is our Lord and Savior. Then we should leave the door open for further discussion.

We have dealt primarily with the ways in which to handle the confrontations one may have with a Person No. 6. They may be many, and they may be heated. However, we can certainly expect that if we do not avoid such confrontations, we will ultimately have an opportunity to talk with this individual about Jesus Christ. Then, of course, the principles we have learned in previous chapters about testimony and witnessing would come into play.

Lest we be discouraged, we should remember that Person No. 6 is probably an individual much closer to accepting Christ than our uninterested friends and relatives. We can help him find the only ultimate Answer.

Study Assignment

Recall the last time you were confronted by a Person No. 6. Write out or act out how you would be able to respond to him now.

Person No. 7

13 *The Nominal Christian*

13 *The Nominal Christian*

Technically, Person No. 7 is a Christian. He has been received into the church in a formal way, was married in the church, and expects a Christian burial. He may come to church several times during the year, but Jesus Christ certainly does not have priority in his life. He may not believe basic tenets of the Christian faith, or he may simply be apathetic. Along with Person No. 3, he may well be the most difficult individual to bring into a living relationship with Jesus Christ.

Here a note of caution is appropriate. As people who would witness to Christ, we must be careful not to put another Christian in the category of Person No. 7 simply because we don't think his brand of Christianity measures up to our own. Person No. 7 is not someone who varies slightly from us in Christian belief or practice. We will misunderstand the suggested means of helping Person No. 7 unless we recognize that he is strictly the nominal Christian and not the Christian brother with whom we are in some shade of theological disagreement.

Particular factors to be taken into consideration in our contact with Person No. 7 are:

1. *One of the basic things to realize about Person No. 7 is that he has probably accepted Christ with his mind but not his heart.* He believes that Christ was the finest person who ever lived, but he has

never fully realized that Christ and God are one, and that therefore Christ should be of primary importance to him. In other words, he has never comprehended the full picture of God coming to be with us in Christ and dying for our personal sins.

Whereas not every nominal Christian falls into this category, the great majority do. Until Person No. 7 can see that Christ died for *him*, he has a limited revelation of God's love. Therefore, we should aim our conversations with him toward a revelation to him that God loved him so much He gave His only Son to die for him.

2. *Jesus Christ is the center of the Christian message.* He is the center of everything. Therefore, in dealing with Person No. 7, we must examine ourselves first to insure that Christ is our message and that it is Christ upon whom we are centering our lives. Unless that is true, we will be of little use in trying to help the nominal Christian take a step of greater commitment to our Lord.

3. *Our contacts with each Person No. 7 can be planned, perhaps to a greater degree than with most of the other people with whom we will come into contact.* In other words, we can make a particular effort to call on the nominal Christian, inviting him into deeper fellowship within the church to which we both belong. This could be a natural occasion for sharing God's love.

Accordingly, we have an opportunity to "do our homework" in preparation for Person No. 7. We can find out from our pastors and others within our church essential background information about this individual. The more we know about him and his interests, the more we can let him know we really care about him. In other words, as we talk with Person No. 7, our knowledge of "public information" about him helps him realize how much we really do care for him. In the lonely and confused world of today, nothing can impress a person more than our being concerned enough about him to know the things important to his life (such as, what his vocation is, how long he has been a member of the church, what offices he may have held within the church, his family, his hobbies, etc.).

Person No. 7 – The Nominal Christian

There are other ways of "doing our homework." We can think through (before visiting Person No. 7) why we want him to come more fully into the fellowship of the church and how we might best be able to convince him to do so. We must realize that we may not be able to give him our testimony or witness, but may be limited simply to encouraging him to come and bring his children to Sunday school and worship services and/or otherwise participate more actively in the church program. Thus, it is important to know what his interests, background, and talents are so we can talk about the things going on in the church which relate to what is important to him.

4. In line with this, if we are calling on a nominal Christian who is a member of our church, *we should be sure that it is not the first call he has received from a member of the church having to do with something other than financial support.* If, despite the time of year and what we say to the contrary, Person No. 7 has never been visited by anyone from the church except on a stewardship canvass, he may not be able to avoid thinking this is the reason we have come to see him. There is a need for the lay people to visit periodically with those church members who are not regular attenders. In that way, people come to see that Christians are not concerned with simply getting the church expenses covered, but are interested in them as individuals.

5. *Needless to say, "sensitivity" is an essential element of visiting Person No. 7.* We must be especially open to the leading of God's Holy Spirit.

If there has been a relatively recent clergy change, he may not like the new clergyman, or he may object to changes in the format of worship services or any number of other things. If possible, it would be helpful to be aware of his particular dissatisfactions before visiting him. Otherwise, through a listening ministry, allow him the opportunity to express to you what problems of this nature he may have. Then be as understanding as possible about his concerns without getting bogged down in them.

Remember that our reason for calling on the nominal Christian is not to argue him out of some petty church problem that might be bothering him, but to lead him toward a commitment of his life to Jesus Christ. We should agree with him, to the extent we can, on petty matters as we move him toward seeing the "big picture."

There are two factors here that deserve special attention. First, Person No. 7 may have some real resentment against the church which, because he has never come to see the whole picture of God's love for him, causes him irritation and frustration. Further, Person No. 7 may assume we have no deeper commitment than he (since he probably does not understand what that would involve), which could cause him to question our motivation in visiting him. That is, he might think it more appropriate for him to be visiting us.

6. *Obviously, we should avoid being judgmental or self-righteous in our relationship with Person No. 7.* He may feel he is "a better Christian" than we are. We must handle our contact with Person No. 7 so delicately that he does not feel we are looking down our pious noses at him. Our love and concern for him have nothing to do with whether he may be a better or worse person than we; we simply have an obligation to lead him toward discovery of what life in Jesus Christ can mean to him.

7. *We should talk in terms the nominal Christian can understand rather than falling into current church or spiritual jargon.* Those of us who are actively engaged in the work of the church tend to forget that we may be picking up terms in our vocabulary not common to the nominal Christian. Unless we are sensitive to that, we will appear to be self-righteous even though we do not intend to be.

8. *We should appreciate the person for what he is and let him know he is missed if he has not been attending our church regularly.* Appeal to him at a level he can understand and capitalize on the fact that individuals do want to be loved and want to feel needed. Our showing that kind of love and concern may be what someday opens the door to allow us to present Person No. 7 with a more complete revelation of Christ.

Person No. 7 – The Nominal Christian

9. *Further, if possible, we must let Person No. 7 know he is important to the broader fellowship of Christ.* In other words, because he calls himself a Christian, he is a part of the body of Christ. Here we are dealing with the possibility that the individual feels he is worshiping God just as much when he is out fishing as when he is in church. If he says such a thing, we might agree with him that it is certainly possible to worship God anywhere, and then add, "But do we? I usually don't. Maybe you do so more than I, but I find that the fellowship of the church and worship in the church are necessary for me to really express to God how grateful I am for what He has done for me."

Another possibility is to say, "Your worship may be complete without us, but our worship isn't complete without you." In other words, it is important to help Person No. 7 see that he is actually a part of a great body of Christians who are in fellowship with one another through identity with Christ, and that we need one another for our worship and service of Him to be complete.

10. *We must avoid telling Person No. 7 what he needs to do.* As far as he is concerned, he doesn't need to do anything.

11. *We should share ourselves freely with the nominal Christian.* We should give of ourselves in Christ's name, letting him know we are ready to help him with any need he may face because we are fellow Christians and love him. If we are not willing to give of ourselves to Person No. 7, he is going to be reluctant to allow our conversation to reach a depth at which any significant breakthrough can be made.

12. *There are, of course, many opportunities to work with Person No. 7 over a period of time.* For instance, the nominal Christian is an ideal one with whom to share books and cassettes that have been meaningful to us. However, as we have cautioned earlier, be sure to share a book or cassette that is only slightly more advanced than where Person No. 7 is at any particular time. If we give him something he considers to be fanatical, we will have seriously impaired our credibility with him.

13. *Also, the nominal Christian gives us an excellent opportunity for*

"secondary evangelism" in encouraging him to come to special events in the church, to visit our prayer group, or to otherwise become engaged in some activity through which he is likely to learn more about Christ.

14. *As a background for helping all nominal Christians within our church, we need to be sure our church provides an opportunity for real Christian fellowship.* If our church is stiff and cold, what are we bringing Person No. 7 into even if we should get him to accept Jesus Christ as his Lord and Savior? We don't mean by this that we should not encourage others to come more fully into the fellowship of our church until we have a body of perfected Christians. God can't wait that long! What we mean is to be sure that there is, within the church, a warm, loving atmosphere sufficient to nurture the person who has come into a fresh relationship with Christ. A small group of dedicated people, willing to give their lives for Christ, can create this atmosphere of fellowship within any church.

15. *Likewise, we should encourage renewal programs in our church* as a part of our "secondary evangelism" efforts to provide Person No. 7 with support, nourishment, and growth.

We could probably go on indefinitely listing factors to be taken into consideration and opportunities available in ministering to Person No. 7. We hope, however, that the above listing has given a sufficient idea of the possibilities. Person No. 7, though he may be one of the most difficult people to lead into a full commitment to Christ, is extremely important to us because he already carries the name "Christian" in the world. To him, we have a special obligation — that he may become what he calls himself.

Study Assignment

Seek out, after prayer for guidance, a lapsed member of your church. Be aware of this person's background. Go in love to visit him, having in mind several of the principles discussed in chapter 13.

14 Sharing God's Love With Our Children

14 Sharing God's Love With Our Children

There are three groups of people who do not fit clearly into the seven categories we have been discussing. Therefore, we are devoting a short chapter to each of these special individuals: our children, a non-Christian spouse, and someone who is in obvious need. This chapter deals with our children.

In talking about sharing God's love with our children, we will concentrate primarily on the family situation. In other words, how do we bring our children into a closer walk with the Lord while they are still "growing up" and a part of the family unit? As Christian parents, we have certain obligations to our children during this time. Some of the matters to be considered on their behalf are:

1. *No one knows us better than our children, and they will be influenced much more by what we are and what we do than by what we say.* Therefore, it is vital that our life style has changed and is changing constantly and consistently as we grow in Christ.

2. *We should not rely on Sunday school to be a major source of Christian nurture for our children.* At most, a child is going to get 10 percent of his Christian education from Sunday school or church. He's going to get the other 90 percent at home, and that

90 percent is going to come from seeing how his parents live.

We need to find good material to use in studying with our children, and we also need to be reading good Christian literature ourselves so that we can increasingly understand the role we are to fulfill as Christian parents.

3. *Further, we should develop faithful habits of prayer, church attendance, and Bible study within the family circle.* We cannot expect our children to have good Christian habits unless we are a part of the formation of those habits. We certainly cannot expect our children to do what we will not do ourselves.

4. *We should share with our children the variety of Christian experiences that should be a continuing part of our lives as Christians.* As God answers prayer in the crises we face, as well as in the simple day-to-day matters, our children should be aware of it. Few things can build a stronger faith in them than coming to know that the family lives a continuing relationship with Christ.

5. *We must be real.* Children have a fantastic ability to sniff out phoniness, particularly on the part of their parents. We shouldn't try to disguise our sinfulness from our children, although we should certainly try to correct it. If we try to build a facade around the way we really are simply to hide our faults from our children, we can only expect them to grow up the same way, perpetuating phoniness for still another generation.

6. *We should let our children know Who is in control of our lives.* If they can see that we continually look to God for guidance, and if they can see that we are humble about our successes and penitent about our failures, they will know we are trying to live according to God's plan for us. The best example and the best training they can have for turning their own lives over to Christ are the personal experiences that we, as their parents, have had in trying to do that very thing.

7. *Also, we should let our children see us in our weaknesses.* When we fall flat on our faces and shed tears of regret, we shouldn't hide this from our children. Although it may be emotionally disturbing for them to see a parent cry, it helps them to better understand the realities of life they must face. Further, as we work

through our failures and our sorrows, we have an opportunity to witness to God's goodness as He provides the forgiveness and the solutions we need.

8. *We should pray with our children on a regular basis.* In this manner, they can see for themselves that God does provide us with what we ask and need. Children can become a part of the ongoing process of communication with God vital to all Christians.

9. *We should pray for the healing of our children, with laying on of hands, when they are sick.* Just as we have an obligation to call the doctor when he is needed, we should be the instrument of God's healing power to the extent that He will use us in this capacity. If we do not think that prayer for our children when they are sick will be helpful to them, how are we to convince our children that they have a loving Father who cares for them and is ready to meet their every need?

10. *We need to be sure that our children have accepted Christ as Lord and Savior;* and it is not inappropriate for us to confront them with the question. If they know we are Christians and that Jesus Christ is the Head of our household, they know that we assume they either have accepted or will accept Christ. We should not assume that they have, but should gently and lovingly put the question to them and, as they are ready, lead them into a relationship with Jesus.

11. *On the other hand, we need to realize that our children belong to God and not to us.* We are charged with specific responsibilities for their upbringing. However, we have to be able to release them to God for His abiding care that He may develop them according to the plan He has for their lives. We should not suppress our children because of selfish patterns we set for them. If we want God's plan for our own lives, we have to let our children find God's plan for them.

12. *We must take time to be with our children and to know their needs.* There was a story in a Chicago paper about a young boy who wrote the sports columnist to ask where he could go fishing. The newspaperman got in touch with the boy's father and said,

"Your little boy wants to know where he can go fishing. Can't you take him?" The father replied, "I've never gone fishing with him. I didn't even know he wanted to go fishing." That was how little time he had for his own son.

One young mother realized the need to cut down on her church activities when the baby-sitter relayed a story to her. The mother said, "We had a baby-sitter for our children about three times a week, and the sitter said something to the children about how much their mother loved them, to which one of the boys replied, 'She loves the church better than she does us.' "

Many books have been written on Christian parenthood, and this brief chapter is not intended to be a substitute for such books. However, in considering the various ways to share God's love, it is essential not to forget our own children. Therefore, we hope the above points will help Christian parents see the specific obligation they have to nurture their children in Christ and to lead them to an acceptance of Him.

Study Assignment

Write out a plan to share Christ in a more meaningful way with your children. Don't neglect taking a good look at things in your life style that need to change.

15 *Sharing God's Love With Our Spouse*

15 Sharing God's Love With Our Spouse

Many Christians find themselves married to a man or woman who falls into the general category of either Person No. 3 or Person No. 7. If we have become Christians after marriage, we may even find that our spouse is Person No. 6. But because of the uniqueness of the marriage relationship, it was deemed advisable to have a separate chapter on special considerations in sharing God's love with our spouse.

Some points we will want to consider are:

1. *As difficult as it may be, we must be willing to surrender our rights and our expectations to God so that He may deal freely with the situation.* Any preconceived notions we have about *how* our spouse should accept Christ are likely to make the situation worse. Such notions tend to bind our partner as he senses what we are trying to do, and he builds up resistance within himself.

We must allow God to work out the matter in His own time. Then we can be open to the ways God may use us as instruments of His grace and not be in constant agony trying to do God's work for Him.

Of course, this process can take a long time. But if we avail ourselves of our own selfish "rights" rather than being willing to sacrifice, we are limiting God. The most effective way God can use us to reach our mates is by our willingness to sacrifice continually. The Christian is the one who should understand that principle and know that God's grace will sustain him through it.

2. *On the other hand, we should not make false assumptions about lack of faith on the part of our spouse.* Because our spouse is a different personality, his or her interest in and response to Christ will manifest itself differently from ours. For example, an active wife may have a quiet husband whose faith is more deeply rooted than hers even though he doesn't talk about it as much or get involved in a multitude of church activities.

3. *We must respect the position of our mate.* We must not belittle our partner's lack of faith in Christ. After all, as a spouse he has certain rights and privileges within the marriage framework and should not be made to feel like a second-class citizen because he has not turned his life over to Christ.

4. *We should work at keeping the lines of communication open.* The more involvement we have with our spouse in the personal ideas, needs, problems, and fears that we face in life, the more likely he is to receive our "communication" of Christ. The strength of the marriage is built upon mutual dependence, and as the marriage is strengthened through open lines of discussion, our loved one is much more likely to be receptive to God's truth.

5. *We must keep our priorities in order, especially family priorities.* If we are living according to the plan God has for our life, it will be increasingly easy for us to determine what is really important and what is not. If we are not showing proper concern for our mate and our children, we are not a good example of walking in the Holy Spirit. On the other hand, as we seek to live in accordance with Christ's desires for us, our spouse can see that this works, and that should intrigue him.

6. In connection with the item immediately above, *we must be particularly careful not to become so involved in church work as to damage the family relationship.* Ros tells the story of the wife who, as she was going out the back door, said to her

children, "You kids can wash the dishes, and I'll be back as soon as church is over." As she left, the remark her husband made brought her to reality: "Why don't you take your bed with you and move over there?" No one is a worse witness than the Christian who neglects his family while he is supposedly doing the work that God called him to do. Although our families may experience some inconveniences from time to time, God does not call us to ministries which wreck our families.

7. *We should encourage separate opportunities for Christian growth within the family.* In other words, we shouldn't expect our mate to come to every prayer or Bible study group of which we are a part. We should encourage him, if that is reasonable, to take advantage of opportunities more specifically formulated for him. In that connection, we should be sure that there are opportunities for study, prayer, and growth available in our church for both men and women.

8. *Finally, where the non-Christian spouse is a man, we should encourage an atmosphere in which he realizes his importance in the family.* That will lead him to realize that he is the spiritual head of the household. When he fully realizes that fact, he is going to feel a responsibility to put his own spiritual life in order.

No earthly relationship is more critical than the one between husband and wife. Clearly, the Christian partner in a marriage could want nothing more than for his spouse to accept Christ. Any of us can think of examples of a Christian husband or wife leading his partner to Christ. Normally, however, that happens as a result of the Christian partner being an indirect witness to the love of God over a period of time rather than a one-time praying with the unsaved partner to receive Christ. Patience is the keynote here.

Study Assignment

Make a list of your *real* priorities as evidenced by what you *do* rather than by what you *say*. Where does your spouse fit on that list? What is the first thing you are going to do about it?

121

16 Sharing God's Love With a Person With an Obvious Need

16

Sharing God's Love With a Person With an Obvious Need

We now look at the last of our special situations. The individual we are concerned with here has an obvious need for physical, emotional, or other help. He may also fall into one of the seven categories dealt with earlier in the book, but his obvious need creates a unique opening for us to share Christ with him.

Therefore, we should consider the following opportunities and factors in attempting to share God's love with the person who has an obvious need, such as illness, loss of a job, death of a loved one, a recent divorce, etc.:

1. *We should empathize with him.* It is only as we share his concern that he can know we really care and, therefore, might be able to help him. Empathy is not something we can turn on and off. We need to be familiar with the problem the individual faces and project ourselves into it that we may know, to some extent, exactly how he feels.

2. *We should avoid "counseling" unless we are specifically asked to do so.* Even then, we should limit our "counseling" to the area within which we have been asked to give help. If the person's problem is of such a nature that he needs professional counsel-

ing, we should lead him to a person who can adequately provide that help.

3. In dealing with any bitterness that may be connected with the need, *we should be careful not to offend the person.* We should be patient with him, love him, and, to the extent possible, identify with him. Quite possibly we have had similar problems in the past and have had to fight bitterness in connection with them. We should be sensitive to his feelings, or his bitterness may erupt in such a manner as to prevent our being of any help.

4. *In this connection, we should help the person to accept himself.* If the problem involves a failure or defeat of some kind, he is likely to have an extremely low opinion of himself. He cannot recover from the problem or even come into a satisfactory relationship with Christ unless he can come to grips with himself. In a loving manner, we may let this person see that he is underrating himself and show him that his defeat or failure is one common to mankind. In His earthly life Christ continually faced many seeming failures of His own which ultimately became part of God's plan.

5. *We must not, however, avoid the fact that the individual must do his part by way of seeking forgiveness and restitution.* It will not benefit him to be unrealistic about what must be done to make things right. Forgiveness from God and from man cannot come unless it is asked for; and where forgiveness from God is needed, there may also lie a need for an appropriate form of restitution. We are short-changing the one we would help unless we are willing to lead him through this entire process.

6. *Because there is an obvious need on the part of this person, we are freer to seek personal information which we must know if we are to help him.* Normally, he will be willing for us to try to understand his problem and will share a great deal of himself in the process. The more information of that kind we can secure, the better we are able to help him by pinpointing his difficulties and leading him, at the proper time, to a decision about Christ.

7. *We should not become so involved in the other person's problems that we forget our God is big enough to handle them all.* We must always be

able to back off and know that God is in control, no matter how entangled the situation may appear to be. He can find some way to lift the individual above it into a new relationship with Him.

8. *As appropriate, we should tell the person, "I'll pray for you."* Then we should do it immediately, preferably in his presence. Through prayer we will gain assistance in helping the person with his problem, and he needs to know that. However, we have to be extremely careful about being phony in saying we are going to pray about a situation. We must really mean it; we should expect something to happen; and we should do it as quickly as possible.

9. *As we pray with the person, we should be sure to admit our own needs so he may better identify with us.* Again, we should not contrive professed needs, but we should pray for those real and natural needs we have that show we, too, are dependent upon God for answers.

10. *Even if the circumstances are such that we must be discussing the person's need with him over the phone, we should not be reluctant to pray.* It is, of course, somewhat awkward to pray with a person over the phone, but it creates no difficulties for God. Therefore, we should consider this just as effective a way of praying about the person's needs as if we were present with him.

It is through knowledge of people experiencing need that Christians are particularly "called to action." We have little excuse for standing around. Not only should we meet the specific need as we can, but we should also see it as an opportunity to share God's love on a broader basis. This special need may be just the means through which God will lead the individual into a personal relationship with Jesus Christ. If so, we might be the instruments through which that is to be accomplished. Therefore, although the above listing is far from complete, it does give us some ideas as to what can be done and how to do it.

Study Assignment

Make a list of people you know who have an obvious need and begin to pray for them. Listen for that inner Voice to know when to make your first move. Even if you go in fear and trembling, God will open the door and use you to help your brother.

17 *More Questions*

17 *More Questions*

There are, of course, multitudes of questions that may still be in our minds concerning the best ways of sharing God's love. We have tried to provide a framework within which we may begin to tell others about Jesus Christ and about God's love for us all. Wherein we have been helped by what we have read, we can be thankful; wherein we have additional questions, they will be answered (and new ones raised) as we practice proclaiming Christ to the seven types of people discussed in this book.

The purpose of this chapter is to try to answer some common questions that have not been dealt with sufficiently in the preceding chapters. Again, we must emphasize that these are not "pat answers," simply suggested ones.

1. What are some "icebreakers" — ways of getting into a conversation with another person about Jesus Christ?

Perhaps an entire book could be written about "icebreakers." We will mention a few just to stimulate your thinking on how you can get into a conversation about Christ with another person.

One method of "icebreaking" is to begin talking about a

subject of general interest: sports, politics, or entertainment. Then, lift the conversation to a higher level by mentioning a well-known Christian in that field and how he or she is witnessing to Jesus Christ.

It is usually easy to get a conversation going on the subject of sickness and health. Then tell about one or more persons you know whom God has healed.

Ask the person about his family and tell him about yours. Then mention spiritual breakthroughs affecting your family. Discuss the healing of relationships brought about by God.

2. My walk with the Lord is still new. I know I will be asked questions I cannot answer. What do I do?

The best solution is simply to realize that people will respect us more if we can be honest and say, "Well, I cannot answer that question either, but I will try to find the answer for you." Then make sure we know what the question is (perhaps write it down) and find the answer as soon as possible.

3. What problems do we face in comparing a person's relationship with his earthly father with that of God as his heavenly Father?

It is a good idea to compare God the Father with the attitudes and actions we might expect from our own father. Yet someday we will run into someone who will say, "My dad was a no-good drunk. What does that make God?" The way to handle that situation is to say, "What would you have wanted your father to be?" Then when he says some things about the ideal father, you can assure him that this is what God is really like.

4. What is the best way to deal with questions about the deity of Christ?

People who are ready to accept Christ do not need a lot of explanation. They can be easily led. However, we will run into people who have serious questions. Often they simply do not believe in the deity of Christ. In that case, one thing we can do is to lead them through the first chapter of John's Gospel, substituting the name "Jesus" wherever we see "Word."

5. Likewise, how do we handle questions about the Trinity?

Many people have trouble understanding the Trinity. It is often helpful to draw a parallel they can understand. One is to show them that the Trinity is like H₂0 which can be in the form of a *vapor* as humidity in the air, in the form of a *liquid* as water, and in the form of a *solid* when it is frozen into ice. Another parallel is to show how a man can be a son, a brother, and a husband — each different responsibilities — and still be the same man.

6. What sort of approaches should we consider in talking with an elderly person about Christ — and a young person about Christ?

When talking with older people, we often find that their need is primarily emotional. Their lives have been shattered by death, by disappointment, or by any number of other things, and they need something in which to believe. Young people often have an intellectual need, and we may need to do more reasoning with them.

7. Isn't repentance an essential part of coming to Christ?

Not necessarily. Many people believe that if we are going to lead others to Christ, we must convince them they are sinners who must be saved. That can be a serious mistake, for this is not our business; it is the work of the Holy Spirit. We can't force repentance on people where that is simply inappropriate. Many people come to Christ because they are overwhelmed with the love being shown to them and not because they are conscious of sins they have been committing. If you tell a person he is a sinner, his natural reaction is to defend himself. Once he is on the defensive, it is extremely hard to show him God's love.

8. Why is it important to center on the person of Christ in talking with an individual?

It is important because we are trying to help the individual come into a personal relationship with Jesus Christ. Unless we have this goal in our minds at all times, we may easily become sidetracked by evasive questions and statements. Moreover, as we center on the person of Christ, it is easier to keep ourselves out of the picture.

9. How do we get people to give us positive answers?

If we want a positive answer, we should ask our questions in such a manner as to evoke a positive reply. It is better to say, "You do want to know more about Jesus Christ, don't you?" than to say, "Do you want to know more about Jesus Christ?" We should assume that the person does and ask the question in such a manner as to encourage a positive response.

10. What do we do about the person who takes the Lord's name in vain?

One problem we all face is how to deal with people who are cursing in our presence, taking the Lord's name in vain. Rather than becoming perturbed at people who do that, we should see this as an opportunity. We can turn to the person using such language and say, "You know, it never occurred to me before, but you have a tremendous God-consciousness." "What do you mean?" they will reply. "Well, His name is in almost every other thing you say. You sure use His name a lot."

11. What about the guy who is involved in some mind-science cult?

What do we say to the individual who says he has found peace of mind through some teacher or book that has nothing to do with Christ? First of all, we need to recognize that if he is sincere in thinking he has found peace of mind, he is not likely to be ready for an acceptance of Christ. However, we can ask him exactly what he does believe about Jesus Christ and see where that opening leads us.

12. How do we promote a good feeling on the part of the person with whom we would share Christ?

One of the most effective ways of showing God's love is to

constantly affirm people where they are and love them for what they are. The more we affirm people, the more they want to give. When we can honestly say, "Yes, you've got a good point there," we are helping the other person to appreciate himself; that will, in turn, help him to appreciate us and what we have to say.

13. Sometimes we will be trying to lead a person to Christ who already knows (in his mind, at least) who Jesus Christ is and what He did for us, and who knows our testimony as well. What can we say to such a person about why he should be a Christian?

Some people have been thoroughly exposed to Christianity all their lives, and they still haven't grasped the truth. They still want to know why they should become Christians. There are many ways to deal with this, as the Holy Spirit guides you. Perhaps one of the best approaches is simply to mention the practical benefits of accepting Christ as Lord and Savior, such as: (a) it is the only way an individual can have a personal relationship with God; (b) you come to see that you are living in eternity with God and that life here on earth is only an "introductory period"; (c) you learn how to live as God intended man to live; and (d) you are able to find ultimate solutions to the problems of life that cannot be found in any other way.

Study Assignment

Create a role-playing situation with two people — you and someone else — being alone together and come up with an "icebreaker." Then evaluate your performance: (a) What was good? (b) What could have been said?

Summary

Summary

For convenience, here is an abbreviated review of each of the seven people and how we can share God's love with them.

Person No. 1

This is the person who is ready to accept Christ as His Lord and Savior. He has discovered Christ through reading a book or during worship services on Sunday morning. He simply wants to know what he needs to do to become a Christian, and we want to be sure he knows what he is doing and help him take that step.

1. We should be able to talk with this person about Christ in our lives: how we came to know Christ, how He changed our lives, and how He is changing us daily. We call this our "testimony."

2. We should be able to tell the person who Christ is, what He did, and why we should believe in Him. This is our "witness."

3. We should be able to lead the person, in prayer, to accept Christ as his personal Lord and Savior.

Person No. 2

This is a person who has shown an interest in our lives as Christians, in Christ Himself, or in the church. We want to help him to come to a decision about Christ, but we must deal with him in a slightly different manner from Person No. 1. We should have in mind all of the background items listed under Person No. 1. Further, we should consider the following:

1. If the person's interest is in the church or in our lives, we should lead him toward (yet wait for) the opportunity to bring Jesus into the conversation in a meaningful way. Remember that there is power in the name of Jesus.

2. We should make sure the individual is absorbing and accepting what we are saying to him by way of our own testimony and witness. Even if he is not ready to accept some or all of the things we are saying, we should be sure he *understands* what we are saying by asking nonthreatening questions and learning his viewpoints as we talk and as we *listen*.

3. We should always leave the door open if we cannot lead the individual through it to an acceptance of Christ. We may do this by saying, "I'd like to talk with you later about this."

Person No. 3

This individual is our uninterested friend or relative. We should first consider why sharing Christ with Person No. 3 is difficult.

1. He knows us too well. (He sees us at our worst, and he knows all the things we have done wrong.)

2. Perhaps we want too badly to share Christ with him.

3. With Person No. 3 we are "prophets without honor." (Perhaps there is a jealousy factor involved.)

4. The very closeness of the relationship between us makes any change in our lives threatening to Person No. 3.

5. Such discussions are also threatening to us because we fear offending our friend or relative.

6. We are supposed to love Person No. 3 anyway; therefore, our special concern for him is not evident as if we were showing such love and concern for a stranger.

7. Perhaps our new life in Christ is not in accordance with the plan Person No. 3 had for us. He is experiencing disappointment with our new direction.

8. With this person, we tend not to have talked about Christ in the past, and now there seems to be a barrier to doing so.

Keeping the above in mind, we should consider preparation and attitudes we need in dealing with Person No. 3.

1. The first thing to do is to question whether our life styles have changed since we accepted Christ and whether they are changing continually as we are molded into Christ's image. Further, we should question whether our lives show consistency in moving in the direction Christ would lead us.

2. We should pray for a supernatural revelation of God to Person No. 3 or through us for his benefit.

3. We should be prepared to wait for a need or crisis arising in his life (such as a severe illness, a disastrous financial setback, family problems, etc.).

4. We should be sensitive to his needs when one of the above experiences occurs.

5. We should pray to be empty of self in our association with Person No. 3, particularly self-righteousness on our part.

6. We can sow seeds of God's love as we have an opportunity to do so.

7. We should recognize the reasons why it is difficult to share Christ with Person No. 3 and find the reasons why there are particular difficulties in dealing with the particular Person No. 3. If, in our past association with this person, we have wronged him in some way, we should seek forgiveness.

8. We should ask God to show us the person's roadblock in accepting Christ, pray for the removal of that roadblock, and wait.

9. We should pray for a surrounding of God's love — not only for Person No. 3, but for ourselves when we are with him.

10. We should be careful not to answer questions we are not asked.

11. We should trust the person to the Lord.

12. We should show consistent love and concern for this person.

Person No. 4

This person is our uninterested neighbor (who is not a personal friend or relative). There are similarities between sharing God's love with him and with Person No. 3. Therefore, virtually all of the points under Person No. 3 also apply to this person. However, some other opportunities exist.

1. We may invite the person into our lives through "outreach projects," such as inviting him to dinner, to do something with us and our family, etc.

2. We should find what is lovable in our neighbor and focus upon that, reaffirming him.

3. We should do something for him and let him do something for us so that we create a feeling of mutual reliance and interdependence.

4. We should be open to hearing his whole problem.

5. We should continually get the message across to him, "God loves you."

6. In any neighborhood controversies that develop, we should be willing to "go the second mile" with our neighbor (surrendering our rights).

7. There is the possibility of a book or cassette ministry to such a person, sharing with him things we have read and heard which we feel will be of interest to him.

8. There is an excellent opportunity for "secondary evangelism." This means we may invite the individual to come to our church, to hear a special speaker, to visit our prayer-share group, etc.

9. We should be prepared to follow up with our neighbor as the light of Christ begins to shine through to him, and particularly after he accepts Christ and needs to be brought into a loving fellowship for continued nurture.

Person No. 5

This is a person with whom we come into contact daily (and

yet who is neither friend nor relative) in our work or as we go about the day; or he may be the person God brings into contact with us (perhaps on a one-time basis) as we sit together with him at lunch, on a plane, or elsewhere.

1. We should consider the significance of external signs and symbols, such as wearing a cross.

2. Whether we are using a Bible or other devotional books can be of significance.

3. If we carry on Christian conversation, this can also be of significance to Person No. 5.

4. By showing a warm, personal interest in Person No. 5, we may be able to develop a conversation that will lead to a discussion about Christ.

5. We may, of course, pray to be led to the prepared heart, in which case God will direct us to those people whom His Holy Spirit has already prepared to hear our message about Christ.

6. We may sow seeds of Christ's love.

7. We have an excellent opportunity for a listening ministry with Person No. 5.

8. We may love people all day long through our eyes, our smiles, and our spirits, if we have prepared ourselves, through prayer, for Christ's love to flow through us.

9. As we sit in a waiting room, restaurant, etc., we have a wonderful opportunity to pray for those around us, asking God to meet their special needs. Often we will notice that the person we are praying for will look up at us and smile or perhaps come over and start a conversation, giving us the opportunity to witness to Jesus Christ.

Person No. 6

This is a person who opposes what we as Christians believe and who, in one way or another, will let us know he opposes us. We should realize that there is more potential in leading this person to Christ than the person who is apathetic. This individual knows he has a need, but he is not presently accepting Christ as the answer to that need because of some prior problem with Christianity or the church. There are some special ways in

143

which we can show God's love to him.

1. We should avoid argument.

2. We need to *listen*, then ask how he reached that viewpoint.

3. We should love him as he talks rather than being busy trying to think of answers to what he is saying.

4. We should expect him to disagree with us.

5. We must not take Person No. 6's attitude personally.

6. We should not defend God. (He can take care of Himself!)

7. We should not avoid encounters with this person.

8. We should sow "God loves you" seeds as we have an opportunity to do so.

9. We should remember that we have the Answer (Christ), but we do not have "all the answers."

10. If the opportunity presents itself, we might ask the question, "Have you ever read the New Testament (or Gospels) in a modern translation?"

11. As we have an opportunity, we should express our belief in Christ so that he knows he has not talked us out of our position. Leave the door open for further discussions.

Person No. 7

This individual is already technically a "Christian" — he has been baptized and confirmed and perhaps attends church occasionally. However, he is strictly nominal in his affiliation with the church. We must deal with this person in a diplomatic manner, because he may believe he is "just as good a Christian as you are."

1. We should realize that Person No. 7 has probably accepted Christ with his mind but not his heart.

2. We should be sure that our life reveals Christ. He is the message. As we center on Christ, perhaps this person will see who the Center is.

3. We can often "do our homework" in preparation for contacts with this person; that is, we should know about him and what his interests are. As we reveal this knowledge in talking with him, he will know we really care about him.

4. If we are calling on a Person No. 7 who is a member of our

church, we should be sure it isn't the first call he has received from a member of the church having to do with something other than financial support.

5. We should be sensitive, following the leading of the Spirit. We should know or discover what may be troubling Person No. 7 about the church (liturgy changes, new pastor, etc.) and be sensitive to it.

6. We should avoid being judgmental, self-righteous, etc., in our relations with this person.

7. We should talk in terms Person No. 7 can understand rather than falling into church or spiritual jargon.

8. We should appreciate the person for himself and let him know he is missed (if he is a member of our congregation and has not been attending church regularly).

9. We should also let Person No. 7 know he is important to the fellowship of Christ.

10. We should avoid telling this person what he needs to do.

11. We should share ourselves freely with him, giving ourselves away in Christ's name.

12. Here, again, is an opportunity for a book and cassette ministry, as we share with him the things that are meaningful to us.

13. Also, there is the opportunity for "secondary evangelism," encouraging Person No. 7 to come to special events at the church.

14. We should be sure that our church provides an opportunity for real Christian fellowship.

15. We should also encourage renewal programs within our church which can help Person No. 7.

Our Children

Here we are dealing with our children while they are still a part of the family unit and while we have certain obligations to them as Christian parents. Some of the matters to consider are:

1. It is most important that our life styles have changed and are changing constantly and consistently as we grow in Christ.

145

No one knows us better than our children, and they will be influenced by what we are and do much more than by what we say.

2. We should recognize our obligations for continuing Christian nurture of our family.

3. We should develop faithful habits of prayer, church attendance, Bible studies, etc., within the family circle.

4. We should share with our children the variety of Christian experiences that should be a continuing part of our lives.

5. We must be genuine.

6. We should let our children know who is in control of our lives.

7. We should let our children see us in our weakness.

8. We should pray with them on a regular basis.

9. We should pray for their healing, with the laying on of hands, when they are sick.

10. We need to be sure that our children have accepted Christ as Lord and Savior.

11. Finally, we should learn to release our children to the Lord rather than trying to possess them for ourselves.

Our Non-Christian Spouse

Either the husband or the wife has accepted Jesus Christ as Lord and Savior and the other has not. Some things to consider are:

1. We (the Christian) should be willing to surrender our rights and expectations so that God can deal freely with the situation.

2. We mustn't make false assumptions about lack of faith on the part of our spouse.

3. We must respect the position of our mate as a husband or wife regardless of his differing religious beliefs.

4. However, we should find ways to communicate with our spouse about personal ideas, needs, problems, fears, etc.

5. We need to keep our priorities in order (especially family priorities).

6. We must beware of becoming too involved in church work to the neglect of the family relationship.

7. We should encourage separate opportunities for Christian growth within the family. In other words, we shouldn't expect our mate to come to the particular prayer or Bible study group we go to, but should encourage him to take advantage of other opportunities. We should make sure that there are opportunities for study, prayer, and growth available in our church for both men and women.

8. We should encourage an atmosphere in which men realize they are the spiritual heads of their households.

Person With an Obvious Need

This is the individual who has an obvious need for physical, emotional, or other help. We should recognize that this is an opening to share Christ with this person — to let Christ meet his needs. Some principles to consider are:

1. We should empathize with him.

2. We should avoid "counseling" unless we are specifically asked to do so, and then we should limit our "counseling" to the area where we have been asked to give help.

3. In dealing with any bitterness that may be connected with the need, we should be careful not to offend the person; we should be patient with him, love him, and, to the extent possible, identify with him.

4. We should help the person accept himself.

5. We should not avoid the issue that the individual must do his part by way of seeking forgiveness, restitution, etc., which may arise out of the need with which he is confronted.

6. We should realize that, because there is an obvious need on the part of this person, we are freer to ask him personal questions than if the need did not exist.

7. We must remember that God is big enough to handle the whole problem.

8. As appropriate, we should tell the person, "I'll pray for

you." Then we should do it immediately, preferably in his presence.

9. As we pray with this person, we should be sure to admit our own needs so that he may identify with us.

10. We should even be willing to pray with him over the telephone, if that is needed.

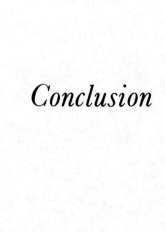

Conclusion

Conclusion

We have now shared God's love with seven types of individuals in several different ways. We have read about the principles involved; we have done our study assignments; and, hopefully, we have found "real life" situations during the period of time we have been using this book.

A person might erroneously conclude that we are to memorize the principles that apply to each of the seven people so we will know exactly what to do in each instance. Nothing could be further from our intent! All of the principles set forth in this book are just common sense — as seen from God's point of view. As we share God's love with multitudes of individuals in the days and years ahead, many of these principles will come to our aid. Further, as we know we are going to visit with Person No. 7, for instance, we may find it helpful to refer to the book and review the principles that apply to that situation. But primarily we should be open to the leading of the Holy Spirit to guide us in what to say and do as we share God's love today and tomorrow, and not be bound to the specific principles listed in this book.

There are only five things we should carry with us from this

151

book as absolute prerequisites for the future:

1. We should always let people know God loves them.

2. Whenever possible, we should bring Jesus Christ into conversations in a meaningful way.

3. We should be able to give our testimony.

4. We should be able to give our witness.

5. We should be able to lead a person, through prayer, to accept Jesus Christ as his Lord and Savior.

As an incentive to do these things, we should consider a story told by a Christian layman, Prime Osborne.

A man, completely "down and out," determined that he would commit suicide because he felt no one ever showed him any love or concern. He decided to walk to the bridge and throw himself into the river. He left himself one loophole: If anyone would show him the slightest amount of love or concern as he walked to the bridge, he would change his mind.

Did that man pass your way?

Appendix

Although not intended to be an exhaustive list, the following passages of Scripture clearly demonstrate the obligation of Christians to proclaim Christ, to witness to Him, and to otherwise share God's love with others:

Matthew	4:19
	10:32
	28:18-20
Mark	5:19
	16:15
Luke	24:45-48
Acts	1:8
	6:7
	8:4
Romans	10:9-15
1 Peter	3:15